Music and Its Secret Influence

Also by Cyril Scott

Occult Books

The Adept of Galilee
The Initiate, Some Impressions of a Great Soul
The Initiate in the New World
The Initiate in the Dark Cycle
The Vision of the Nazarene
An Outline of Modern Occultism
The Greater Awareness
The Boy Who Saw True (Introduction, Afterword, and Notes)

Philosophical Books

The Real Tolerance
The Art of Making a Perfect Husband
Childishness: A Study in Adult Conduct
Man is my Theme
Man the Unruly Child
The Christian Paradox

Autobiography

My Years of Indiscretion
Bone of Contention

Health Books and Pamphlets

Doctors, Disease and Health
Victory over Cancer without Radium or Surgery
Health, Diet and Commonsense
Simpler and Safe Remedies for Grievous Ills
Medicine, Rational and Irrational
Cider Vinegar: Nature's Great Health-Promoter
Crude Black Molasses, the Natural 'Wonder-Food'
Constipation and Commonsense
Sleeplessness, Its Prevention and Cure

Poetry

The Shadows of Silence and the Songs of Yesterday
The Grave of Eros and the Book of Mournful Melodies
with Dreams from the East
The Voice of the Ancient
The Vales of Unity
The Celestial Aftermath

Music and Its Secret Influence

Throughout the Ages

Cyril Scott

With a new introduction by Desmond Scott

Inner Traditions
Rochester, Vermont • Toronto, Canada

Inner Traditions
One Park Street
Rochester, Vermont 05767
www.InnerTraditions.com

Originally published in the United Kingdom in 1933 by Rider & Co. under the title *Music:
Its Secret Influence throughout the Ages*
Second, expanded edition published in 1950 by Rider & Co.
Third edition published in 1958 by Rider & Co.
Fourth edition published in 1969 by Samuel Weiser Inc., New York, NY
Fifth edition published in 2013 by Inner Traditions

Library of Congress Cataloging-in-Publication Data

Scott, Cyril, 1879–1970.
  Music and its secret influence throughout the ages / Cyril Scott ; with a new introduction
by Desmond Scott. — 5th ed.
    p. cm.
Includes bibliographical references and index.
ISBN 978-1-59477-487-4 (pbk.) — ISBN 978-1-59477-498-0 (e-book)
1. Music, Influence of. 2. Music—History and criticism. 3. Theosophy. I. Title.
ML3920.S366 2013
781.1'7—dc23
                                                              2012027928

Printed and bound in the United States

10 9 8 7 6 5 4 3

Text design and layout by Priscilla Baker
This book was typeset in Garamond Premier Pro with Delphin and Altast Greeting used as
display typefaces

This book is gratefully dedicated to

MASTER KOOT HOOMI LAL SINGH

and to the memory of his pupil

NELSA CHAPLIN

ontents

⌒

PART I
Preliminary
What Is Inspiration?

PART IV

Historical

Melody and Harmony from Pre-Egyptian Times
to Nineteenth-Century England

PART V

Some Occult Prognostications

Toward Beauty and Mystery

Introduction

It seemed right to use this introduction, not to discuss the reissue of a book that has seldom been out of print since it was first published in 1933, but to present a brief overview of the life and career of composer, author, and poet, Cyril Scott. It is hoped it will provide some context to his work, and allow readers who have not encountered him before a greater understanding of how and why this book and many of his others came to be written.

Scott was a man with one single aim in this incarnation. Whether composing music, or in his occult books discussing the workings of the Masters and recounting his impressions of a Great Soul, whether advocating alternative medicine or writing beautiful poetry, his intent and hope was always to help humanity along the path of spiritual evolution.

There are those who know Cyril Scott solely through his music, and in particular for a haunting, exotic piece called *Lotus Land*.

There are those who know him solely as the author of the Initiate trilogy and other occult books.

Then there are those who know Scott solely as the author of books on alternative medicine, of which he was a pioneer decades before it became mainstream—books such as *Doctors, Disease and Health* (1938) and *Victory over Cancer* (1939), which got him into trouble with the orthodox medical profession because he dared to suggest there might be other ways to deal with cancer than by radiation, which was then considered the only possible treatment.

Believing strongly that cures for many diseases were best obtained by natural means, not drugs, he produced other books, too, such as *Simpler and Safer Remedies for Grievous Ills* and the enormously popular pamphlets on cider vinegar and black molasses.

A multi-talented man, he was also a poet, producing seven volumes between 1905 and 1915 (including two translations, one from the German, the other from the French), and a final one almost thirty years later, in 1943, which contains some of the best verse he ever wrote.

As if that weren't enough, or if inspiration had failed, for relaxation he painted; imaginary dawn and sunset landscapes with hills, trees, and water in pinks, purples, and blues.

Music and Its Secret Influence combines three of his abiding interests—occultism, music, and healing; healing because the genesis of the book occurred at a place of healing and the literary midwife, Nelsa Chaplin, was a gifted healer there.

More of that later, but first some background on Cyril Scott.

He was born to a middle class, church-going Protestant family in the north of England. As a child growing up near Liverpool, the horse and the railway were the only means of locomotion. It was a world we wouldn't recognise today, one where Queen Victoria was firmly on the throne and the British Empire was at its height. It was without cars, planes, radio, TV, DVDs, computers, or the Internet, but in 1969, a year before he died, he sat in front of the television and watched a man land on the moon. That's quite a change in one lifetime! His father was a businessman involved in shipping, whose chief interest was the study of Greek. His mother played the piano "with a certain superficial brilliance, and had even written a waltz which somehow got into print."

As a young child he was abnormally sensitive and precocious, bursting into tears at any music that affected him. He played the piano almost before he could talk, picking out tunes from the barrel organs heard in the street outside.

When he was twelve, his parents sent him to the Hoch Conservatorium in Frankfurt to study piano, where he was the youngest pupil accepted up to that time. He stayed there for eighteen months, came home, decided he was more interested in composition than in teaching or being a concert pianist, and returned to the conservatory when he was not quite seventeen. There he heard Clara Schumann play and remembered vividly getting the day off when all his professors went to Berlin for Brahms' funeral in 1897.

Success came early to Scott; his first symphony was performed in Darmstadt in 1900, his second in London in 1903. The year 1903 also saw the first performance of the Piano Quartet, in which the famous Fritz Kreisler played the violin part, which, as Scott wrote, "brought my name before the (London) public in a manner which, short of murder, nothing else could have done."

Though at the beginning of the twentieth century Scott was hailed as "The father of modern British music," by the time of his death in 1970 he had been almost forgotten. Very little music was being performed, and none recorded.

Now, (2012) the Wheel of Fortune has turned again. Interest in him has never been higher.

All the solo piano music is available on CD as are the major orchestral works. Notices have been uniformly enthusiastic and a reviewer described the third symphony, *The Muses,* as "A remarkable discovery in twentieth-century British music."

At sixteen, reacting against the conventional Christianity of his parents, and shortly before returning to the Conservatory he became an agnostic.

If there were no God to bother about, to placate and sing doggerel hymns to, if death were simply the cessation of consciousness, how preferable that seemed than worrying desperately whether you would go to hell or not when you died!

But around 1905, well-established in London, composing and

playing his own compositions, he went one evening to listen to a lecture on theosophy. Though not totally converted, he was much impressed by its ideas. Not long after, he came across a book called *Raja Yoga* by Swami Vivekananda and from then on, as he tells in the early autobiography, *My Years of Indiscretion,* "The study of all forms of mysticism and transcendental philosophy became for me a passion; and not only that, but I found in their study a new and great source of musical inspiration." From both Theosophy and Vedanta he leaned that there are many different approaches to God, and all are valid.

Our real nature is divine. God exists in every living thing, and religion is a search for self-knowledge, a search for the divine within ourselves.

From there, too, he learned about a Hierarchy of Initiates, initially from reading and later from personal experience. This experience he recounts in three books: *The Initiate* (1920), *The Initiate in the New World* (1927), and the *Initiate in the Dark Cycle* (1932). They were first published anonymously by "His Pupil," because what mattered, Scott insisted, was not the messenger but the message, and he only later acknowledged them as his when it became impossible to remain anonymous any longer.

The subtitle of *The Initiate* is *Some Impressions of a Great Soul,* and in it and the subsequent two books he tells of his meetings with those whom he believed were themselves Initiates.

Transcendental mysticism, or Occultism, which Scott described as a blend of science, philosophy, and religion, teaches that every living thing is in the process of evolving, from lower to higher states of physical and spiritual existence. This process in all its phases is guided by a great Hierarchy of Initiates. Initiates are those who through long and sustained endeavour have attained these higher states. Purified of baser emotions such as jealousy and selfishness, and filled with love for their fellow beings, they work ceaselessly to guide others along the same path that they themselves have trod. It is important to stress that they act only as *guides,* never dictate but simply suggest, and never attempt to coerce or compel.

They are people like us, not angels or demi-gods, and differ from the rest of us only in *degree,* not in kind. The doctrine of reincarnation is implicit here, since no individual could possibly be expected to reach even comparative perfection in one short life.

Occultism also teaches that the whole Universe is an expression of energy, and that not only the elements, but all beings both embodied and disembodied are storehouses and transformers of energy. Karma, the law of cause and effect, governs the entire cosmos, both visible and invisible. Cyril Scott discusses this in much greater detail in his book *An Outline of Modern Occultism* (1935).

Music and Its Secret Influence first appeared in 1933 under the title, *Music: Its Secret Influence throughout the Ages.* It is dedicated to Master Koot Hoomi Lal Singh and to the memory of his pupil, Nelsa Chaplin. Nelsa Chaplin, who died in 1927, was a brilliant psychic who was able both to see and to hear disembodied entities, such as Koot Hoomi, or Master K. H., whom she had been in touch with since her childhood. She and her husband Alex Chapman ran a rest-house called "The Firs," which specialized in treating people for a variety of different, hard-to-cure ailments.

For some years, beginning around 1919, Cyril Scott had been going there periodically, and it was there that he met his wife, Rose Allatini, whom he married in 1921. Rose was a talented novelist who wrote under a variety of pseudonyms including Eunice Buckley, the name by which she later became best known.

She shared his interest in occultism and reincarnation, and one of her early novels, written under R. Allatini before she met Scott, was titled *When I Was Queen in Babylon.* Koot Hoomi was also her Master.

This is how Scott, both in his autobiography *Bone of Contention* (1969) and in the later editions of the book itself describes the way it happened: "While my wife and I were staying at *The Firs,* Master K. H., one Sunday, intimated that the time had come when it was desirable to make known the esoteric aspects of music, and that the Masters wished to use my pen to that end. 'I will,' he said, 'give the data to the little one (as he called Mrs. C.) and *you* will work them out in detail.' Thereafter a time was set aside when Nelsa would get into rapport with the Master, and while she clairaudiently listened to the data he gave, I would make notes to be worked out later. After I had completed a few chapters, I would read them to her while she would listen for any comments or corrections the Master might wish to make."

Scott adds emphatically that he had previously no idea about the occult effects of music whatsoever.

He also remarks on another occasion that it was immaterial to the Masters what kind of person you were, all that mattered to them was your suitability for the task at hand and implied no particular merit or virtue on your part.

Music is generally thought of as being reflective of the age in which it is produced, and this is true of the majority of cases and of most pop music in particular, but there are instances, this provocative book suggests, where music is no mirror but instead is an instrument of change. Scott discusses a number of composers, Bach, Handel, Beethoven, Mendelssohn, Schumann, and others who, consciously or unconsciously, were guided to write by the Masters. The one he singles out above all, though, is Richard Wagner. Fully aware of the unfortunate effects his music led to, such as uncritical hero-worship and excessive German nationalism, Scott nevertheless writes: "The keynote to Wagner's music-drama is unity in diversity. In the old-fashioned opera each number—involving a different melody—was separate and apart; but with Wagner . . . , although there are a vast array of themes, melodies and *motifs*, they are woven together to present one continuous whole. A profound spiritual principle underlay his entire scheme—the many were blended together in the one. As the waves of the ocean are each different, yet are one with it and inseparable from it, so each melody was one with the great art-work of which it formed a part. Wagner's music was the prototype of the principle of co-operation against competition; symbolically speaking it symbolized the mystic truth that each individual soul is unified with the All-soul, the All-pervading Consciousness."

Other occult books Scott produced were *The Vision of the Nazarene,* which discusses the original teachings of Jesus, and how those teachings have been misunderstood over the ages, and *The Greater Awareness,* which is a sequel to the *Outline of Modern Occultism.* It concentrates on the practical, rather than the theoretical side, arguing that love influences every aspect of our lives, from romantic attraction and matrimony to humour and self-knowledge.

One of the most widely read of Scott's occult books, however, is his last one, *The Boy Who Saw True* (1953).

This is the account of a clairvoyant boy's childhood in Victorian England in the 1880s. It is an amusing and delightful work but conceals a more serious purpose, covering much of the same ground as in The Initiate books but approaching it from the innocent viewpoint of a child.

Since that first encounter with Master K. H., Scott felt he was continuously guided by him and sought his advice on all-important decisions.

In 1943, for instance, during WWII when he was sixty-three, he was at a very low ebb, no longer sought after as a composer, short of money, depressed, and unwell. He felt death to be near but Master K. H. told him he had more work to do, and so he continued—for the next twenty-five years! During that time he produced not only a number of chamber works, trios, quartets, and quintets but also major works including his only full-length opera, *Maureen O'Mara,* a large secular oratorio, the fourth symphony, the second piano concerto, an oboe concerto, a concertino for flute and bassoon, and a sinfonietta for organ, harp, and strings.

Whether it was analyzing Wagner's music that struck him so forcibly or whether the idea was communicated to him by Master K. H. during the writing of *Music: Its Secret Influence throughout the Ages,* the concept of unity in diversity became his passion and his credo thereafter.

As early as 1932, before the *Music* book was out, he composed and wrote the libretto for a *Mystic Ode,* which in its original title was called *Ode to Unity.* He also explores in his verse the belief that we are all on the same journey toward enlightenment, though each of us is at a different stage on the road.

Here is the last stanza from a long poem written during WWII. It is called "If He Should Speak Today" and though the speaker is never named we may assume Christ or a high Initiate is intended.

> *So am I always nigh to those who seek for me*
> *Upon the plains or scan the mountain's peak for me,*
> *It matters nothing what their creed or caste may be*
> *All noble strivings lead at last to me.*
> *Some selfless souls I guide have hardly heard my name,*
> *No man however often he has erred, I blame;*
> *For Love Divine all things forgives because it comprehends*
> *Those sins that fret the pilgrim ere his arduous journey ends.*
> *And if I do not stand before your errors dumb,*
> *'Tis this, and only this—*
> *That through self-knowing all the swifter ye may come,*
> *Responsive to my call,*
> *To share that never to be quenchéd Bliss,*
> *Which is the heritage of all.*

His plea for unity in diversity found its fullest expression in 1946–7 when he composed his great Universalist choral work, the *Hymn of Unity*. He didn't begin work on it until he had consulted the Master and got his approval. He then wrote the libretto in about three weeks, and completed the whole hour-long oratorio in six months, fully aware that it was most unlikely ever to be performed in his lifetime. In both words and music it sums up his entire philosophy and expresses everything he believed in and strove for all his life. This is the final chorus:

> *O LIFE that men do call by divers names*
> *And cry to thee as Brahman, God, or Great White Spirit.*
> *O thou whose nature and whose name is Love.*
> *And by the power of Love dost hold all things together,*

And who dost dwell in us as we in Thee:
O grant that we may manifest a greater measure of thy Love
And may perceive at last the saving, mystic truth
That with each other we are One, as we are one with Thee!
Oh, may the spirit of that Unity irradiate our hearts
So that the dark and deadly sin of separateness
May vanish like the night when morning wakes,
And that the Age of Brotherhood may dawn and may
endure for Man.

Those lines are as relevant, and as much needed now, as they were when he first set them down over sixty years ago.

DESMOND SCOTT

Desmond Scott is the son of Cyril Scott and the administrator of the Cyril Scott estate. He is a graduate of Cambridge University and is a director, actor, and sculptor who has acted and directed in England, Canada, and the United States. Since 1999 he has been giving lectures on his father in England, the United States, Canada, and Australia.

PART I
Preliminary
What Is Inspiration?

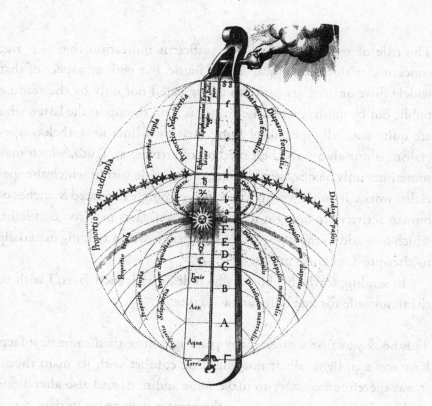

Preface

The title of this book should be sufficient indication that it is not concerned with the technical side of music, but with an aspect of that widely disseminated art hitherto unsuspected not only by the reading public but by musicians themselves. This is no slur upon the latter, who are quite naturally specialists along their own line; nevertheless, specialism is not always the best method of arriving at Truth, which may sometimes only be discoverable outside the circle within which the specialist works. In other words, when two seemingly unrelated branches of human activity are brought into conjunction, facts may come to light, which may add to the sum-total of knowledge, whilst tending materially to alter previous conceptions.

In sending forth this book, which deals with such facts, I wish to thank my wife for much literary assistance.

This book was first written many years ago, since then some new facts have come to light, albeit not ones that conflict with its main thesis. It was therefore necessary to make some additions and also alterations to the original text so as to bring the present volume up to date. Some of those personalities figuring in the earliest editions having died, allusions to them in the present tense became no longer applicable; whilst the names of a few others who have also died, would bear little significance for the reader of today. Furthermore, vast changes are occurring and have already occurred in the world of man, seeing that we have just emerged from the Piscean Age and have entered a new one, namely the Aquarian Age. Altogether, we live in a time of transition. Even present-day music itself is in a transition state; though some contemporary composers may not wish to think so.

The writer hopes that by bringing the book up to date, he has thus contrived to improve it.

I $\mathcal{T}$he Problem of Musicality

There are certain phases of human activity, which may appear quite simple and straightforward on the surface, but which, when carefully scrutinized, confront us with manifold problems, complications, and paradoxes. The less we think about them the more we imagine we know about them; and the more we think about them the less we realize we know about them. Custom has prompted mankind to regard music as an art and a means of affording enjoyment through sound to all such as respond to its charms; but of its exact nature and the scope of its influence we are strangely ignorant. We accept music, discuss music and matters musical much as we accept and discuss life and all pertaining to it; yet what life *is* no one as yet has revealed. Life is a mystery to those who trouble to think about it, but merely a fact to those who do not; the same may be said of music. It is not merely a combination and succession of sounds, but a mysterious something, which, as we will endeavour to show, has exercised a powerful influence throughout the ages.

Yet in attempting to enlarge our conception of music itself, it were as well at the outset to rid ourselves of certain *misconceptions* regarding the nature of musicality. It is advisable to know to some extent our position relative to this vexed problem, for, owing partly to the inaccuracies of our language, the epithet "musical" is bandied about with a pronounced disregard for its true meaning; the one word being pressed into service for a large variety of interpretations. In spite of an array of philosophers who might be credited with enriching the language, the Germans likewise are limited to the one adjective *musikalisch,* which bears exactly the same meaning, or rather lack of definite meaning, as our English "musical." As for the French, they are compelled to use a phrase, which is not grammatically reproducible in our own language; they say of a man *il est très musicien,* which, adjusted to grammatical needs, would run: "He is very (much of a) musician." In Italian the same idiom obtains, and both phrases suggest rather the realm of complimentary utterance than that of logical truth. A man is either a musician or not a musician, just as a man is either a Frenchman or not a Frenchman; to be obliged to say, therefore, that a man is very much of a musician, when one may really mean that he is not a professional musician at all, but only resembles one, denotes a poverty of language that is very misleading. But even more misleading is the ambiguity with which both the words "musical" and "unmusical" have become endowed. Leaving aside poetical utterance, investigations have shown that there are no less than twenty-five different interpretations of these epithets, of which some examples may here be adduced.

A man is often termed "musical" who has a mild liking for claptrap music: (a) by a person who has no liking for music of any kind himself; (b) by a person who also likes claptrap music and hence considers that he also is musical. Or again a man may be termed "musical" who enjoys so-called low-brow music but dislikes classical music; who enjoys classical music but can neither play nor sing himself; who can play and sing a little but dislikes classical music; who occupies himself much with his wireless set, but is really more interested in the wavelengths than the music.

As regards the term "unmusical," a man who only cares for "trashy music," or by courtesy "music of an immediately fascinating order," is often termed unmusical by the man who only cares for what is known as classical music; a man who only enjoys classical music is often termed unmusical by a man who enjoys modern music; a man who merely "knows what he likes" is invariably termed unmusical by the professional musician and even the layman; people who only care for vocal music are often termed unmusical by musicians other than singers; singers are often termed "an unmusical race" by newspaper critics because they are not always on the note and are sometimes more preoccupied with mere voice-production than interpretation; *virtuosi* are often termed unmusical because some of them are more preoccupied with what is effective than with what is high art.

It will be seen from the foregoing that accurate definitions of the words "musical" and "unmusical" may be sought for in vain, and that their whole significance is so elastic as to be dependent on personal opinion rather than on specific standards. For the purpose of this book, therefore, we may dismiss the negative side of the problem and regard all persons as in varying degrees musical who react to music and hence, as will be shown, are influenced by music in varying ways.

There are, of course, a number of people who hold very definite ideas as to what is and what is not music, but these people need not detain us. To dismiss as "not music" all compositions, which appear to them ugly or incomprehensible, may be satisfying to themselves; but such a dogmatic attitude is of no special interest to others. From the standpoint of these pages, all forms of composition—from the most primitive folk song to the most elaborate and discordant examples— must be regarded as music. Nevertheless, it is of some interest to speculate as to whether certain phases of music evoke a purely musical reaction or involve other factors of which the listener is unaware. A few reflections on the nature of pure music and the psychology of soloism may serve to throw some light on the subject.

2

The Problems of Pure Music and Soloism

By the term "pure music" we do not, of course, refer to a type, which might be of especial interest to moralists, but to that form, which makes an exclusively musical appeal, or is colloquially described as "music pure and simple." The terms absolute or abstract music do not serve us, because they are employed to denote the opposite of programme music; and although we shall show later that vocal music is a form of the latter, it is incorrect to imply that instrumental soloism is also a form of it. Our immediate object is to show that even so-termed abstract music may derive some of its interest from external things; therefore, it is not entirely pure.

Now, if we are hazardous enough to express a doubt as to whether soloism, in whatsoever form, constitutes pure music, we wish to say at the outset that no unflattering aspersions are cast upon soloists as such. When, for example, we can say of a woman that she is not only clever but also beautiful, we are not saying what is uncomplimentary, but what is doubly complimentary: we imply that she makes a twofold appeal. And that soloism in a like manner makes a twofold appeal or even a multifold appeal must be patent to all who have thought on the subject. Leaving aside all other considerations, there are two points, which engage the attention of an audience; the one relates to the *matter*, the other to the *manner.* With a certain type of audience it is not of importance *what* the soloist performs, but *how* he performs it—in a word—such an audience does not go to hear the composition; it goes to hear the soloist.

It is stating the obvious to say that star soloists draw the largest and most mixed audiences, but the members of those audiences themselves are for the most part unaware of the reason—namely—that the enjoyment they derive is not wholly a musical one: it is in part the result of seeing a given person make a successful effort!

This admiration for the process of effort-making on the part of others appears to be latent in the entire human race. It explains the popularity of acrobats, dancers, football-players, pugilists, and the like. It explains why a crowd collects to watch horses dragging a heavy wagon up an almost impossible hill; it also explains the admiration for all virtuosity. The vociferous applause, which follows a *bravura* piece at the end of a piano recital, is not because that piece was the greatest on the programme, but because the pianist was using the greatest effort to play it. The high C with which a tenor may finish a song is greeted with deafening applause not because a high C is more beautiful than a low one—it is often less so—but because the tenor is putting forward the maximum of effort, concealed or otherwise, to produce it. Again, loud music is not intrinsically more beautiful than soft, yet the former nearly always evokes more applause than the latter, partly because it requires more effort to produce. The same applies to florid music in contradistinction to slow music, and this helps to explain the prodigious success of virtuosity.

All this goes to show why the soloist makes a multifold appeal, and, if famous, draws the largest audiences. As the making of a successful effort is considered synonymous with being clever, those persons who are not especially attracted by music as such, may be attracted by cleverness. They are like certain men who, having little eye for feminine beauty, can nevertheless enjoy the society of a beautiful woman if she is intelligent. Such men, however, as goes without saying, do not reap the full benefit of her attractiveness; they are the victims of their own limitations.

Of the various types of soloism, vocal soloism is in a sense the furthest removed from pure music, and this is because all singing derives a part of its interest from something external, as previously implied. Although songs without words do literally exist, they are exceptional, and hence not only words—but all they portray—must be taken into account when considering vocal music.

Thus, the singer who is a great artist is a twofold artist; he (or she) possesses both musical and histrionic capabilities. Effective singing is a form of oratory, just as effective oratory is a form of music. A great orator needs to be not only something of an actor, but also to possess an ear for melodious utterance and rhythm; a great singer needs to be an orator, an actor, and a musician all in one. Nevertheless, the conjunction of words with music is taken so much as a matter of course that people seldom look upon songs as anything but pure music. Our contention, therefore, that all vocal composing and rendering constitute a species of programme-music may seem extravagant both to the professional and the lay mind. Yet can one maintain that the appeal made by a song like *Home, Sweet Home* is a purely musical appeal? It obviously makes a domestico-sentimental one to all those in whom it does not provoke feelings of distaste. It has even been sung by singers with hardly any voice left to sing it; and despite the fact, brought tears to the eyes of the lachrymosely inclined. *Home, Sweet Home* is a stroke not of musical but of sentimental genius; it is furthermore a noteworthy example of a perfect synthesis between the quality of the music and the quality of the words. Neither is of value if judged by the standard of high art, yet rendered by vocalists with histrionic ingenuity they conjointly moved audiences for over half a century.

All the same, some songs are more "programmistic" than others. There are songs that relate stories in the words *actually* and in the music *imitatively;* and there are those that portray emotion or atmosphere only. Both these types are well known. A third, which was prevalent in the Victorian and pre-Victorian eras, has more or less died out; its chief characteristic was tautology and hence artificiality, as was very noticeable in the arias of Handel, Meyerbeer, and others. To say that there was no connection at all between the words and the music would be going too far, but there was certainly very little. The reason why the aforesaid composers, with their verbal repetitions up and down the scale, produced such an artificial effect was quite obviously because for one thing they were attempting the impossible; they attempted to turn vocal music into pure music, and only succeeded, partially and artificially, in turning pure music into vocal music. This attempt is no longer made nowadays, because we live in a less artificial age, when too glaring incongruities are not tolerated, at any rate in serious art, though they still survive in such entertainments as musical comedies.

Although I am perhaps the first writer to point out that all vocal music is a form of programme music, there are many indications to show that the fact has been realized subconsciously—hence, the two surviving classes of song I have mentioned. Vocal music, having become more imitative and thus more congruous, coloratura songs are now only written (though there may be exceptions) when they possess some raison d'être—an imitation of birds or other florid sounds of nature. As for non-coloratura songs, the better type are nearly all atmosphere-producing (also a form of imitativeness), the voice-part tending more and more towards the declamatory, as witness in the songs of Debussy, Ravel, and others.

There are two forms of imitation in vocal music: imitation of inflection and imitation of any sounds to which the poem alludes. By imitation of inflection is meant an endeavour to reproduce in music the inflection of the voice if a given poem were being recited or spoken. As regards this, even renowned composers have shown lapses of taste, either because they have possessed no dramatic instinct or else a faulty and illogical one. True dramatic effects are brought about by means of inflection and not by imitation. Therefore, a composer who is a true artist endeavours that his melody shall enhance inflection, and he does not detract from the effect produced by the addition of imitative melodramatic by-play in the accompaniment. To write imitative music that is worthy of the name of art, it is essential to be imitative in a new way—a very difficult matter—and also to be consistent and congruous.

Moreover, a judicious suggestiveness is usually more artistic than realism. The better type of imitative songwriters like Debussy and Ravel adopted this method: they used their accompaniments to create a species of stage-setting for what is to be sung.

Until the enrichment of harmonic device, song composers were solely dependent on their singers for the reproduction of the varying emotions that the poems demanded. As there were comparatively few discords, a concord had oftentimes to do service for the imitation of an ugly or a forcible emotion. In ballads, for example, the self-same accompaniment was frequently employed for any number of verses, although the emotional content of those verses was widely divergent. Thus, the accompaniment part of a song gave no dramatic assistance to its vocal interpreter. But nowadays an enlightened composer will employ a variety of harmonic devices to express a corresponding variety of emotions, whether he alters the melody or not. To give added expression to a harsh or ugly emotion he will write a harsh or, relatively speaking, ugly discord; to give added expression to a tender emotion he will write a tender-sounding harmony, and so forth. Another device is to alter perhaps one note of the melody to suit an altered inflection of voice demanded by a particular word occurring in verses other than the first.

It is unnecessary to pursue this train of thought further. Granted that songs are a species of programme music, and that audiences may be attracted towards concert halls for reasons not wholly associated with pure music, the fact remains that they are influenced to a greater or lesser degree by such music as they may hear: though how and why will be explained later.

3

The Problems of Inspiration and Invention

Which brings us to one of the most important aspects of musicality invention itself, and all that it denotes and involves. And here, according to some of the more fastidious composers, we shall be treading on delicate or sacred ground, at least, so it would appear from utterances or silences of some composers who were requested to define the nature of inspiration. To quote the actual words of one of them: "The great difficulty of an inquiry of this kind is that some not unnaturally look upon it as an impertinent curiosity, as an endeavour to tear asunder the veil that shrouds the Sanctum Sanctorum of their art." Yet why should they thus look upon it? Inspiration may be mysterious in one sense, but that does not render it too sacred to be analyzed—as far as analysis is possible. Inspiration is, at any rate, usually associated with beauty, and what is beautiful is worth the attempt to comprehend, however difficult the task may be.

Mr. James Branch Cabell, in his volume *Straws and Prayer-Books*, so perfectly expressed the *rationale* of creative writing that even though his remarks apply to literature, they may with some trifling adjustment equally apply to musical composition . . . "The novelist," he main-

tains, "will write in the form . . . which he personally finds alluring, his
rhythms will be such as caress his personal pair of ears; and the scope
of his writing will be settled by what he personally does or does not
find interesting. For the serious prose craftsman will write primarily
to divert himself with a part, thrifty but in the main a philanthropic
under-thought of handing on . . . the playthings . . . which he contrives,
for the diversion of those with a like taste in anodynes. And to do this
will content him." Mr. Cabell then goes on to say that there is upon
him a resistless hunger to escape from use and wont; that he seems more
utterly resolved than are his fellows not to be bored; and that, therefore,
it is his endeavour to avoid the tedium of familiar things.

Now if we transfer all these observations from the plane of literary
composition to that of musical, we shall understand at any rate the more
immediately *apparent* reason why a composer composes. Quite baldly
and unequivocally stated, composition pleases him. If he is a bad composer, it results in his pleasing himself only; if he is a good composer, it
results in pleasing others, either immediately or in the course of time.
One may even measure the greatness of a composer by his capacity for
being dissatisfied, for example, with the familiar. Mediocre composers
are satisfied with second-hand ideas, great composers are only satisfied
with first-hand ideas, and their consistent greatness is partly dependent
on their patience in striving to obtain those ideas. To say that genius
is the infinite capacity for taking pains is therefore only to state the
second half of the truth, the first half being that genius is the infinite
capacity for feeling dissatisfied. I grant that both these statements need
to be taken *cum grano salis,* but considering that geniuses, apart from
their work, are often highly impatient, the second half of the truth, as
I state it, is approximately as correct as the first. Comparison with bad
or inexperienced composers* serves to emphasise this fact. The young
woman who discovers she can, after a fashion, compose, will often take
the resultant song or whatnot more seriously and delightsomely than a
genius takes his latest masterpiece. That seriousness and delight may, in

---

*For obvious reasons I omit those who do hack work solely for money.

a small measure, be due to vanity, but for the most part it is due to an all too easily attained feeling of satisfaction relative to musical ideas; this, stated otherwise, simply implies a proportionate incapacity for feeling bored. And yet a certain love for a type of novelty is the cause of that satisfaction. Now and then to write a song provides a *new* sensation for our hypothetical young woman, and that is why it delights her; but from an artistic point of view her effort is valueless, because coincident with an aspect of novelty that proves boring to all but herself. She typifies, in fact, the difference between the master musician and the nonentity: the master musician composes to please himself and succeeds in pleasing others; the nonentity composes to please himself and fails to please others, or at any rate those whose opinion is of worth. Some nonentities, however, compose in the hope of pleasing others, not so much in order unselfishly to give them enjoyment as to reap their approbation. This does not necessarily spring from vanity but from fear—they need encouragement—for they fear that without it the flower of their new delight, the capacity to compose, may wither and die.

Thus, the whole compositional process is a reaching out after what one personally likes; piscatorially expressed it is a fishing for ideas calculated to give one personal pleasure or delight. The prerequisite for this desideratum is that they should be different, varied, otherwise *new* ideas, for repeatedly to catch the same ideas would be to a composer as tedious as for a fisherman repeatedly to catch the same fish—if the simile be pardoned.

How does a composer fish for ideas? He improvises in his head or on the piano until he strikes something, or something strikes him, which he happens to like; when this occurs, he writes it down, and having done so, resumes his fishing. The Germans have an expressive phrase for this "striking" process; they say *"Es fällt ihm etwas ein,"* which, literally translated, means "something falls into him." But it stands to reason that nothing could "fall into him" unless he held himself receptive or opened his mind to catch it; the "fishing process," therefore, is simply a process of opening the mind.* When a composer

---

*Sometimes ideas strike him, even when he is not actively holding himself receptive, but these moments are comparatively rare.

settles down to work, he in reality settles down to "fish," and if he is in good form, and his mind is clear, he then catches or contacts ideas that are of value to him. When, to the contrary, he is not in good form, he only catches the commonplace, which, if he possesses the adequate sense of dissatisfaction with the familiar he at once rejects.

Now there are various types of ideas which, in the course of his fishing, may strike a given composer: those which, being complete in themselves, lead nowhere, and those that lead to a large number of further possibilities. Thus, there are ideas connected with phrase, scales, or modes; ideas connected with device; ideas connected with structure or form; and ideas connected with harmony. For example, a composer may hit upon what is at any rate to *him* a new chord, and having done so, finds to his satisfaction that that chord is employable in a hitherto unthought-of variety of ways. He can build all kinds of melodic structures over that one chord; he can even use it to form melody itself, as Brahms used his octave-and-a-third device. And so he employs that one chord in this, that, and the other manner until a moment arrives when it entirely ceases to please him; it has grown familiar to his aural sense; in brief, he has become wearied by it and hankers again after something *new*. Consequently, he once more starts the fishing process, and if he is fortunate his efforts are rewarded with success; if not, he wisely ceases his attempts, enters on a drab period, and tells himself that he is "not in the mood" to compose.

And he who possesses that species of temperament, which is content to follow the line of least mental resistance, will be content to accept Mood as the cause of both productivity and unproductivity. He will probably tell us that infertile moods are the result of inertia, indigestion, mental fatigue, or any other physical cause; and that fertile moods are conversely the result of good health or being in good form. Nevertheless, this hypothesis is not watertight, for the simple reason that some great works have been written during periods of ill-health and much physical or mental pain or stress. Beethoven composed with remarkable assiduity at times when everything conspired to upset him. Mendelssohn, on the other hand, could only compose effectively when the river of life ran a smooth and even course. Some creative artists, whether musical or literary, have obtained their best inspiration during the throes of an unhappy love affair; not so others—in such circumstances—they have merely languished. Happy love affairs, on the contrary, have galvanized them into producing great art.

Some people have even so far confounded cause and effect as to maintain that dyspepsia is responsible for pessimistic philosophy, but in point of fact, the dyspepsia can only be responsible for the pessimism and not for the philosophy itself. Philosophers like Carlyle are not evolved merely through the eating of indigestible food, nor are poets like Dowson evolved merely through unrequited passions for barmaids. Romantic passion is a physical-mental phenomenon, and although in given circumstances it may produce poetry, it does not produce *poets*— otherwise poets would be more plentiful. On the contrary, it is the poet who produces the romantic passion; he poeticalises the barmaid in his own mind, and then falls in love with her. . . . All of which goes to show that the prime cause of creative or uncreative moods can be neither a purely physical nor a purely emotional one—in the sense of the physical or emotional influencing the mind in such a manner as to produce or inhibit inspiration. In a word, physical and emotional causes are secondary causes, the true cause being far more recondite.

4

Inspired and Uninspired Composers

Since the earlier editions of this book were published, certain things have come to light, which go to substantiate much that is later on stated in these pages. Therefore, so as not to augment the present volume to undue proportions, the data on hand may be put forward in place of what I previously wrote.

Four months before his death, Brahms, for one, made the confession that when composing, he felt himself to be inspired by a Power external to himself. Believing as he did in One Supreme Spirit, he maintained that only when the creative artist was receptive to that Spirit could he and did he write immortal works, and not otherwise. This was tantamount to saying that all truly great artists, in whatever field, are mediums, whether conscious of the fact or not. I may add in passing that when Brahms made his confession, he stipulated that it should not be published until fifty years after his death; hence, it has not figured in any biography.[1]

Nevertheless, it has now belatedly been revealed that Brahms was one of those composers who believed in inspiration of a more special kind than do those sceptics who only believe in what they can see, hear, taste, feel, or smell. It has been argued by such persons, and even by some others, that a composer is the outcome and, in a sense, the expression and reflection of the age in which he lives. This, however, according to the esoteric facts is only a half-truth. For roughly speaking there are two types of composers; those we may refer to as the inspired ones, in that they possess qualities that permit of their being used by the Higher Powers, and as opposed to these, the uninspired ones, who, lacking such qualities, cannot be used as mediums. Briefly stated, the inspired composer, as will be shown in the course of this book, is he who through the medium of musical vibration and expression helps to mould the characteristics of the future, whereas the uninspired composer, for the most part, merely reflects those of his own times. This explains why so much of present-day music and that of recent years (I write in 1958) is of the ultra-discordant species—for are we not and have we not been living in a highly discordant and contentious age? There is also this to be said; the uninspired composer, in contradistinction to the inspired one, is usually swayed by prevailing musical fashions, and instead of creating his own idiom is apt to be influenced by one or other of the "Schools," be it for instance Neoclassicism, the Twelve-Note System, or what not. The dictum, therefore, that a composer is the outcome of his age is not entirely untrue if by that is meant the majority of composers, whether regarded as "highbrow" or not. But it is untrue if it means all composers, thus excluding those comparatively rare ones who are endowed with more than mere cleverness and whose music is not a reflection of the things "earth earthy" but of the "things of the spirit." I am aware that in speaking of certain creative musicians as being inspired, although the term may convey something vaguely to religiously minded people, it conveys nothing to the materialist. Yet materialism offers no convincing explanation for that mysterious charm, that elusive *something* which renders a number of works of art immortal. Nor can materialism or even orthodox religion convincingly account for genius. It is only Esotericism which affords a satisfying explanation.

5 *The Esoteric Source of This Book*

When some years ago I wrote from the esoteric standpoint a book called *The Influence of Music on History and Morals,* I was faced with many difficulties that time and the trend of opinion have subsequently diminished. During recent years occult ideas in one form or another have become widely disseminated, and scepticism toward the not immediately explainable or perceptible has ceased to be the fashion among the intelligentsia. Spiritualism has recruited an ever-increasing number of adherents; some theosophical ideas have been embraced even by nontheosophists; astrology finds its place in the daily papers; reincarnation and Karma (the law of cause and effect) have been accepted as logical doctrines, while the higher types of clairvoyance, clairaudience, and kindred faculties are no longer treated as subjects for ridicule and pseudo-sapient negation. Christianity is also undergoing changes, and the recognition of an esoteric or hidden side to its many pronouncements is ever growing wider. Even science is becoming more occult—though the scientists themselves may object to the term—for the recognition of hidden forces plays an important part in modern scientific conclusions.

All this being so, in putting forth this new book, in which, however, I embody such portions of the old as are indispensable to the basic argument, I am enabled to dispense with many of those dissertations on the rationale of occult science itself, which aimed at enlightening the general public, but which could only prove irksome because already familiar to occultists of various schools. For instance I was constrained emphatically to argue the actual existence of that Hierarchy of Great Sages, Initiates, Adepts, known as the Great White Lodge (see chapter 16) which exercises such a mighty influence over the evolution of mankind. But in the interim the *Mahatma Letters to A. P. Sinnett*[1] have appeared, and also a notable book, *Through the Eyes of the Masters* by David Anrias,[2] which testify to the fact that these mysterious Sages were *not* the invention of that much-maligned occultist, Madame Blavatsky, but have been, and can be, contacted by all those who are prepared to develop the necessary, though with difficulty, attainable qualifications. The result, both direct and indirect, of these books and others of a similar trend,[3] has been to dispel that feeling of opposition, which so often arises in the minds of sceptically disposed people when confronted with ideas or facts with which they are entirely unfamiliar. This is partly because ideas, floating about, so to say, in the mental atmosphere, filter through to the subconscious before they are apprehended by the objective mind. As the psycho-analyst implies, it is not the conscious brain that resists a new idea, but the subconscious—a condition, which is altered when forces of thought have repeatedly impinged upon it, and, like eddies of water in connection with a stone, have worn away its resistance. In a word, that ignorant and complacent antagonism towards new revelations has perceptibly waned, as also the exaltation of mere belief as opposed to knowledge. Consequently, the ground has been prepared for what has been given me to set forth in this new volume. For although in *The Influence of Music on History and Morals* I stated unequivocally that I was indebted to a high Initiate of Esoteric Science for all my information regarding the hidden effects of music, I was not permitted to disclose his name—the time not being ripe—nor yet that of the remarkable seer who clairaudiently received that information and passed it on to me to be expounded and elaborated. Fortunately, however, this injunction has now been rescinded, and I am in a position to acknowledge my indebtedness to the Master Koot Hoomi, who was my Authority for what was previously set forth and for much added information which follows. This High Initiate, who I may mention *en passant* resides in Shigatse, takes a special interest in the evolution of Western music, a fact which theosophical literature has failed to stress, even though He was one of the two sponsors of the Theosophical Society at its inception—towards the end of the last century.* Indeed, He considers it advisable that students of occultism of all schools should more fully appreciate the great importance of music as a force in spiritual evolution, and to this end He has revealed much that has hitherto not been revealed, and that cannot fail to prove of paramount interest to all music-lovers.

Yet at the time when I wrote my first book on this subject, nothing could have been achieved without the instrumentality of His pupil, Nelsa Chaplin,† a highly trained clairvoyant of unusual sensitiveness who, since her earliest days, had been in close telepathic contact with Master Koot Hoomi. This remarkable seeress was nonetheless remarkable because her name is not to be found among those of psychics who have attained recognition. Her true spirituality was such that she gave freely of her gifts, yet never turned them to mundane account nor indeed exploited them in any way whatsoever, as our brief outline of her history will show.

Born of elderly parents, from her earliest years she possessed supernormal faculties, among which was the power to leave her body and transport herself in spirit to the higher planes as well as to physical-plane localities thousands of miles away. She remembered, for instance, as a mere child having been frequently transported to Master Koot Hoomi's house at Shigatse in the Himalayas, where on many occasions she listened to those improvisations on the organ that form a part of His many and varied activities. But apart from these spiritual transportations, or so-termed astral projections, she possessed the faculty of "tuning-in" to the Master's thoughts, a faculty, which would seem well-nigh incomprehensible to the lay mind, did not Wireless bear to it so close an analogy.

---

*Readers are reminded that Theosophy is no sect or new-fangled religion, but the synthesis of Science, Philosophy, and Religion in its most all-embracive sense.

†A pen-portrait of her under the name of "Christabel Portman" has appeared in *The Initiate in the Dark Cycle,* by His Pupil.

For the fact of invisible thought-currents vibrating through the ether and "picked up" by brains sufficiently sensitive is, although on a different plane, in itself no more and no less miraculous and mysterious than the fact that the vibrations of a Beethoven Symphony from Prague or Rome may be carried through the ether and heard by listeners in outlying villages in England! All is vibration of varying grades. On the plane of mentality, Adepts living in complete seclusion are able to communicate with Their equals, disciples and pupils thousands of miles away, provided the "receiving-stations" are properly attuned.

And that Nelsa Chaplin was one of those whose delicately poised mental equipment was so attuned I have already implied. Moreover, she was remarkable in other ways. She had evinced a precocity, which enabled her at an unusually early age, not only to read and appreciate such works as those of Dickens, but to play and improvise upon the piano in a most phenomenal manner. Phenomenal, also, in their accuracy and scope were those clairvoyant and clairaudient faculties, which made this strange little being seem such an enigma to many in her environment. Her affinity with birds and flowers, the facility with which she appeared to be able to contact the essence of music itself, proclaimed her almost more of a fairy than a normal child. But completely unselfconscious and unable to realize that others could not see and hear what she could, the possession of her psychic gifts in particular was often a cause of misunderstanding and jealousy. Yet though her sensitive nature suffered much in consequence, the directing influence of her Master saved her from the spiritual and psychic blindness that has been the fate of many other perceptive children misunderstood by unimaginative elders.

As she grew up her faculties became augmented and perfected. Through her improvisations she conveyed, in terms of music, states of soul-consciousness, or even such harmonies as she might hear when she beheld a beautiful sunset: for to one so unusually endowed, a sunset may be audible as well as visible. And sometimes Master Koot Hoomi would actually *play through* her, when He desired to achieve some special— usually healing—effect on those under her care. For it should be mentioned that during a number of years she was associated with a species of guesthouse which, in connection with her husband and a doctor, was run mostly for the treatment of strange and obstinate diseases, many of which had baffled more orthodox medical practitioners. A system of colour-healing had been evolved under the direction of the Masters,* and very remarkable were some of the results achieved in regard to those diseases, which were usually found to be psychological in origin, and to involve the subtler bodies. Here it was that Nelsa Chaplin's clairvoyant faculties of diagnosis proved so invaluable; and in addition, on all those who suffered both in mind and body she showered a sympathy and an understanding, which in themselves were healing balm, to many a friendless or world-battered soul. Great indeed the solace and spiritual wisdom she dispensed to those tormented by doubts, complexes, and fears; and when she was baffled as to what line to take with a given patient, it was to the voice of her Master that she listened for guidance and direction.

For a great honour was hers: both the Master Koot Hoomi and the Master Jesus frequently overshadowed her and used her as Their medium. (It should here be mentioned that the Master Jesus is particularly interested in those occupied in the work of healing.) She told me how one day for the first time she had experienced the wonderful sensation of being lifted out of her body by Master Koot Hoomi, and how, as she stood by His side in her spiritual body, she saw Him controlling her physically in order to speak to her husband and the doctor.

Many of the patients, however, had never even heard of Masters, except perhaps in a vague way, and were content to regard Mrs. Chaplin merely as a lovable personality with a wonderful gift of intuition; while some of those who were Theosophists, holding the idea that all communion with the Masters is exclusively reserved for Leaders of the Society, never suspected how close her contact with Them actually was.

It may pertinently be asked why one so uniquely endowed should, even despite her natural reticence, not have come before the notice of,

---

*Throughout this book I refer to The Masters in capital letters, not because They would wish it, for They modestly regard Themselves as "the elder brothers of humanity," but out of deference to theosophists, who thus refer to Them in their literature.

at any rate, her fellow initiates;* and the answer is that it was not her destiny in this particular incarnation thus to be recognized and publicly acclaimed. Rather was it intended that her life—as indeed that of most advanced initiates unless they have some specific mission in the outside world—should be one of self-sacrifice made in comparative obscurity. And that well-nigh incessant suffering was her portion, all those who knew her intimately are fully aware. Her whole being was so responsive to the harmonies of the higher spheres, as well as of this one, that it had been her great longing to devote herself entirely to music: to convey in earthly sounds some echo of those celestial ones to which she was so subtly attuned. Yet there was other and less congenial work to be done, for the sake of which this longing had very largely to be set aside, and only given expression on those rare occasions, which I have mentioned. Furthermore, she had to contend against a perpetually ailing body, against poverty, worry, and tormenting problems of numerous kinds; even against envy and jealousy for which she, in her modesty and simplicity, could never account.

Nevertheless, she lived and suffered not only heroically, uncomplainingly, but joyously until the end: joyously, in that her consciousness, even while she struggled with earthly difficulties, was almost permanently at one with the joy of the Higher Ones.

My own association with Nelsa Chaplin extended over a period of seven years, and during that time on many occasions Master Koot Hoomi spoke to me through her, giving of His pearls of wisdom and instructing me as to how I could best serve the Great White Lodge, not only by my music, but also by my pen. It was on one of these occasions that He told me the time had come when it was desirable that mankind should be enlightened regarding the esoteric effects of music and its influence upon well-nigh every phase of civilisation. He then asked me to write a book on the subject, with the aid of His pupil acting as His medium.

Thereafter, a time was set aside when Nelsa Chaplin would get into

---

*Broadly speaking, initiation confers the power to respond to higher and higher rates of vibration and states of consciousness.

rapport with the Master, and while she clairaudiently listened to the data He gave, I would make notes to be worked out in detail later on. Sometimes she would require to look up the Akashic Records since certain parts of the book dealt with eras long ante-dating history. At others she would answer the many questions I had perforce to ask regarding this or that difficult point. After I had completed a few chapters, I would read them to her while she would listen for any comments or corrections the Master might wish to make. In this way the book came to be written, inspired, and sponsored by Him who in a former life had been the great philosopher and musician, Pythagoras the Sage.

My contact with Master K. H., though temporarily interrupted, did not end with Nelsa Chaplin's death. The Masters of Wisdom possess the power to materialise a body in any part of the world so as to give instructions or convey messages to Their pupils. And by these means, after some others had been used in the interim, my contact with the Master was eventually re-established.

I should here mention that when the Masters of Wisdom inspire the writing of a particular book, They watch with Their far-seeing spiritual eyes over its faring in the world, so that They may gauge the effect it produces both individually and collectively. They come to perceive which portions are assimilated and which rejected, either because they fail to excite interest or because the majority of readers are not yet in a position to comprehend them. Moreover, temperament and the characteristics of the age have to be taken into account. People of today—very different from their predecessors—require everything in as condensed a form as possible. That "speeding-up" noticeable in so many departments of life has not failed to react on certain branches of literature. Therefore, some amendments and curtailments have been made in such portions of the original book as I have incorporated in this present one, and much new material has been added in accordance with the Master's wishes.*

---

*The record of past events are impressed upon the ether, and only to be deciphered by highly trained clairvoyants.

6

The Effects of Sound and Music

*The influence of music on the development of religion is a
subject which would repay a sympathetic study.*

SIR JAMES GEORGE FRAZER: *THE GOLDEN BOUGH*

Throughout the ages, philosophers, religionists, and savants have realised the supreme importance of sound. In the Vedas, said to be the oldest scriptures in the world, it is stated that the whole cosmos was brought into manifestation through the agency of sound. And, later on, the author of St. John's Gospel expressed, in effect, the same truth, when he wrote: "In the beginning was the Word, and the Word was with God, and the Word was God." The writer of the Book of Joshua must also have possessed some knowledge of the power of sound; otherwise it is unlikely that he would have written the story of the Fall of Jericho.

It has been proved that sound can be both constructive and destructive: it can create forms, it can also destroy forms. From a chaotic sprinkling of sand on a glass plate, geometrical patterns may be formed with the aid of a violin bow drawn across the edge of the plate; a fact that proves the constructive effect of sound vibrations. Conversely, the

36

sound of the human voice may be employed to shatter a tumbler or wine glass to atoms.

And, apart from this, it is patent to everyone who has given the subject a moment's thought that it is to sound we originally owe our power to communicate one with another. This power, in its most elementary form, is first perceived in the animal: it reaches its culmination in the speech of Man. From speech to the most elementary form of song was but a step, and, with the taking of that step, music came into being.

And if sound in itself is of such importance, what may be said of it when blended and mellowed to form the art of music? For an answer, let us turn to one of the greatest thinkers of all times. "Musical training," writes Plato, "is a more potent instrument than any other, because rhythm and harmony find their way into the inward places of the soul, on which they mightily fasten, imparting grace, and making the soul of him who is rightly educated, graceful." So pronounced, indeed, was Plato's opinion of the effects of music that in another part of his *Republic* he says: "The introduction of a new kind of music" (this also included poetry and dancing) "must be shunned as imperiling the whole State: since styles of music are never disturbed without affecting the most important political institutions." Nor was Plato alone in his opinion, for Aristotle undoubtedly shared it when he wrote:

Emotions of any kind are produced by melody and rhythm; therefore by music a man *becomes accustomed* [italics mine] to feeling the right emotions; *music has thus the power to form character,* and the various kinds of music based on the various modes, may be distinguished by their effects on character—one, for example—working in the direction of melancholy, another of effeminacy; one encouraging abandonment, another self-control, another enthusiasm, and so on through the series.

Such, then, were the opinions of these ancient philosophers whose writings have long survived the dust of Time. Yet, although they so

forcibly expressed themselves relative to the comparatively simple music
of their day, it seems to have struck very few writers, let alone the laymen of our present generation, that various types of a music far more
complex, far more powerful, possess qualities other than purely artistic, pleasure-giving, transiently soul-stirring or conversely soothing.
For years music lovers have listened to the oratorios of Handel, to the
symphonies of Beethoven, to the etudes of Chopin, and to the operas
of Wagner, and have realised that each of those master-musicians has
created a special individual style, and that a Beethoven symphony is an
entirely different work of art from an oratorio of Handel. Nevertheless,
not one of these music-lovers appears to have credited either Handel or
Beethoven with exercising a definite and general influence on character and morals; and, no doubt, if they have read Plato's views on music
and its effects, they will merely have considered him the victim of an
erstwhile superstition. Yet that such a notion was erroneous we hope to
prove in the following pages.

We purpose, in fact, to show that each specific type of music has
exercised a pronounced effect on history, on morals, and on culture;
that music—however horrifying this statement may appear to the
orthodox—is a more potent force in the moulding of character than
religious creeds, precepts, or moral philosophies; for although these latter show the desirability of certain qualities, it is music that facilitates
their acquisition.

A little reflection on the subject must bring us to the conclusion
that music operates on the mind and emotions of man through the
medium of *suggestion*. To paraphrase Aristotle's statement, if we repeatedly hear melancholy music, we tend to become melancholy; if we hear
gay music, we tend to become gay, and so forth. Thus the particular
emotion, which a given piece of music depicts, is reproduced in ourselves; it operates through the law of correspondences. Furthermore,
our researches have proved to us that not only the emotional content
but the essence of the actual musical *form* (see chapter 32) tends to
reproduce itself in human conduct; hence, we may with justification
formulate the following axiom—*as in music, so in life*. And it is very

important that the reader should bear this axiom in mind in considering all that follows.

Psychological investigation has proved that by the repetition of a formula suggesting physical or moral qualities, those qualities can actually be acquired. A case in point is the application of M. Coué's formula: "Day by day in every way I get better and better." And it should be noted that the more quiescent the patient, the more efficacious the suggestion, for in the quiescent state, the spirit of opposition has no occasion to assert itself. Music is a species of formula, with the additional advantage of not being expressed in words, which could arouse this spirit of opposition, we do not, of course, refer to songs. It is so insidious that it *suggests* while the listener remains unaware of the fact.* All that he realizes is that it awakens certain emotions, and that in degree those same emotions are always awakened by the same or similar musical compositions. Music, therefore, is constantly *suggesting* to him states of emotion and reproducing them in him, and as *emotional* habits are as readily formed as, or even more readily than, other habits, they eventually become a part of his character. It is obvious that Aristotle was aware of this when he wrote that "by music a man *becomes accustomed* to feeling the right emotions."

But we do not intend to imply that music operates on the emotions only: there are several types of music that operate on the mind. Thus, we shall see in due course that Bach's music had a very definite effect on the mentality—for, in accordance with our axiom—as Bach's art is of an intellectual type, it produces an intellectual effect.

But the question arises, has music, at any rate in the past, been sufficiently disseminated to bring about such prodigious effects on mankind in general as are claimed for it in this book? How can music have influenced collective thought, unless so widely diffused as to operate directly on the greater bulk of humanity: have there not been vast numbers of

---

*Why the results of "musical suggestion" are not so specific and concentrated as those of ordinary suggestion is obvious. A man may confine himself to the repetition of one formula for months, but he may hear hundreds of varying types of music during the same period.

people who seldom, if ever, heard music of a serious character? Yet although the question is pertinent, it is easily answered. History shows that rulers and leaders of thought—and it is these who are chiefly concerned—have nearly always been in contact with some form of music. Kings, dukes, popes, and princes have had their "court musicians"; feudal lords and barons have had their bards, while the masses have at any rate had their folk music. From the most ancient times, wherever there has been any degree of civilisation, music has played a role of more or less importance. And the following point should be emphasised: that wherever the greatest variety of musical styles has obtained, there the adherence to tradition and custom has been proportionately less marked; and where musical styles are limited, as, for instance, in China, adherence to—nay, even worship of—tradition obtains to a marked degree. We are fully aware that in stating this we would seem to be lending weight to the prevalent notion that styles of music are merely the outcome and expression of civilisations and national feelings—that is to say, that the civilisation comes first, and its characteristic species of music afterwards. But an examination of history proves the truth to be exactly the reverse: an innovation in musical style has invariably been followed by an innovation in politics and morals. And, what is more, as our chapters on Egypt and Greece will show, the decline of music in those two instances was followed by the complete decline of the Egyptian and Grecian civilisations themselves.

There is one more point to be noted in this preliminary chapter. We have to take into account that element in the masses which causes them to reflect or absorb the opinions of others, whether those others be leaders or merely characters more forceful than themselves. Thus, even in times when music of every description was not broadcast as it is today, assuming that a number of people never heard a note of music at all—which is unlikely—they were nonetheless influenced *indirectly* by it, and this also applies to the frankly unmusical. Consequently, a large portion of this book is concerned as much with the indirect effects of music as with the direct ones. For instance, the direct influence of Handel's music was, among other things, to inspire awe and reverence, but the indirect effects were, as we shall see, to engender some of the less agreeable characteristics of the Victorian era.

It is our task to show the various ramifications, outcroppings, by-products, and composite influences of music in general, from the earliest times to the present day. But, for reasons of expediency, we propose to deviate from the usual course of "beginning at the beginning," and, instead, to commence with those comparatively recent master musicians dating from Handel. This inverted procedure has been adopted because, whereas the reader is likely to be familiar with comparatively recent music, and hence in a better position to follow the argument, he is less likely to be familiar with ancient music. However, when once the premise has been accepted he will have no difficulty in following cause and effect in relation to that music with which he is not actually familiar.

To summarise: Music affects the minds and emotions of mankind. It affects them either consciously or subconsciously, or both. It affects them through the medium of suggestion and reiteration. It affects them either directly, indirectly, or both; hence, as in music, so in life.

I should finally add, that when describing the various effects that the music of the master-musicians had on humanity, that is not to say that every single piece they composed was instrumental in producing those effects; the latter were produced by their most inspired and individual works.

PART II

Biographical, Analytical, Aesthetical

The Influence of Genius on Daily Life

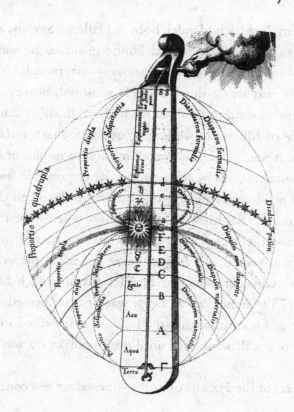

7

George Frederick Handel and the Victorian Era

In 1710, Georg Friedrich Händel, born at Halle, in Saxony, and known to the English as "Handel," visited London; but, as he was under an engagement to the Elector of Hanover—afterward George I of England—his visit was a short one. He returned, however, in 1712; from that time onward until his death he lived in this country, and to the influence of his music we largely owe the characteristics of the Victorian era. It was, in fact, his exalted mission to revolutionise the state of English morals; it was he who came to be responsible for the swing of the moral pendulum from the one extreme of laxity to the other of undue constraint. That his works should have taken some time to bear fruit is because the higher type of music is less speedy in its results than the lighter-veined; the former being less often played. We must also take into consideration that Handel did not reach his maturity until about 1739, when *Israel in Egypt* was first performed. It is, therefore, no matter for surprise that the full and many-sided influences of his music were not disseminated until the Victorian era was well under way.

The effects of the Handel oratorio—for we are less concerned with his other works—were the awakening of reverence and awe with all their concomitants and consequences. The nature of these latter will be understood when we say that it is largely, though indirectly, owing to Handel that the Victorian age was so steeped in conventions, and that many of its people were prudish, punctilious, and tainted with priggishness. But these undesirable attributes must be regarded as the defects of *qualities,* as the inevitable result of Handel's influence on certain temperaments. There *are* people to whom moderation of any sort is unknown, which should be borne in mind, when considering the contents of this chapter.

In writing a book of this nature, it is important that all considerations of personal taste and preference should be excluded; it is for this reason that we make no apology for citing the opinions of others in connection with those composers under review. But we have further reasons: it is essential to obtain some idea of how those great creative talents were regarded at an earlier epoch than that at which we write, at an epoch when the elaborations and complexities of more modern composers were unknown. In other words, how did Handel strike the people of that era, which he was instrumental in moulding? To answer this question, we will quote from a series of lectures delivered by a noted divine of the Victorian period.

The works of Haydn, he maintained, of Beethoven, Mozart, Mendelssohn, Spohr, and others—great masters!—are performed, and they are admired, and justly so, but they have not the hold upon the taste and feelings (of Englishmen at least) that Handel has. He is the greatest and the favourite. He stands alone. His great productions are unaffected by time. The vicissitudes caused by varying fashions, by changing tastes, or changing schools, are temporary. We cannot conceive the possibility of any human composition permanently taking the place of the *Messiah*. There has of late years been a great revival of taste for high music, but the more high music is cultivated, the more marked amongst great composers is the supremacy of Handel.

To state as briefly as possible the general grounds on which I argue the merits of Handel as a composer, I should say they are—first, the majesty and sublimity with which he treats his subjects; second, his great power in pathos; and third, generally in an exquisite *appropriateness* of his music to the words he has set.[1]

But if these eulogies go to prove the esteem in which his works were held, the following encomium, from the pen of a contemporary Mus. Doc., is even more significant.

The choruses, he writes, making comparisons favorable to Handel, of Mozart and Beethoven are frequently *magnificent,* but seldom *sublime.*[2] It is, in fact, the sublimity of Handel's music which impressed so forcibly his many admirers. Other composers may at times be grand and powerful, as the reverend lecturer we have first quoted continues, but they lack the *simple* grandeur with which Handel can bring forth his ideas. . . . He produces some of his most touching and most sublime effects by efforts which are wonderfully simple. . . . Now . . . it is a mark of real power and of very elevated capacity for a composer to produce what is great art and at the same time simple.

These eloquent tributes to Handel's awe-and-reverence awakening influence might be multiplied, but we will be content with two other citations, one from the *Quarterly Review,* the other from Dr. Gregory's biography of the Rev. Robert Hall.

We feel, runs the first of these on returning from hearing the *Messiah,* as if we had shaken off some of our dirt and dross, as if the world were not so much with us; our hearts are elevated, and yet subdued, as if the glow of some action, or the grace of some noble principle, had passed over us. We are conscious of having indulged in an enthusiasm, which cannot lead us astray, of tasting a pleasure, which is not of the forbidden tree, for it is the only one, which is distinctly promised, to be translated with us from earth to heaven.

Nor is the second citation in its own way less pregnant with meaning.

Mr. Hall it runs was present in Westminster Abbey at Handel's commemoration. The King, George III, and his family were in attendance. At one part of the performance of the *Messiah* (the "Hallelujah chorus") the King stood up, a signal for the whole audience to rise; he was shedding tears. Nothing, said Robert Hall, had ever affected him more strongly; it seemed like a great act of national assent to the fundamental truths of religion.[3]

So much then for the general and essential influence of Handel's music. We will now deal with those outcroppings already mentioned, and their cause.

Those who have closely examined Handel's technique will observe that he had a strong predilection for the repetition of single chords, for two or more bar phrases, and for *sequences*—viz.: the reiteration of a phrase in a different position or on a different degree of the scale. Thus, apart from its emotional content, Handel's music was preeminently formal in character, consequently it was formal in effect. If, however, we combine its emotional qualities with its formalism, and to repetition and musical imitativeness—for sequence is but imitativeness— add grandeur, the net result is the glorification of repetition and imitativeness; and if we translate all this from the plane of music to that of human conduct, we get love of outward ceremony and adherence to convention. For, after all, what is conventionalism? It is simply the glorification, however, unconscious, of imitativeness. As a musical sequence is the imitation of a phrase under slightly different *musical* circumstances, so is conventionalism the imitation of other people's thoughts and actions under slightly different *material* circumstances. But to this conventionalism we have still to add the feelings of awe and reverence mentioned at the beginning of the chapter, and the net result is veneration for tradition, a degree of Puritanism and all that accrues from it: in certain conditions ugliness, gloom, pietism, over-punctilious observance of the Sabbath, and so forth.

Yet, in enumerating these less beautiful and less direct effects of Handel's genius, these Victorian characteristics, which in the twentieth century we have come to regard with a degree of amusement if not contempt, we must not forget how necessary they were as a corrective at the time. Handel flourished in England during the era when Swift, Sterne, and Smollett were writing their breezy obscenities, and when reverence even for sacred things was an almost negligible quantity. Although religion was preached and formed part of the national life, it was certainly not coordinated with spirituality. The sporting *bon vivant* type of parson was not only tolerated, but afforded by his actions no perceptible discrepancy between religion and worldliness. Thus, both Swift and Sterne were in orders, but that did not so prevent them from being "licentious, coarse-minded men," as their Victorian biographers described them, nor, in spite of, or perhaps because of, their coarseness, from acquiring great literary fame. But what a change was to come over the whole aspect of things, clerical and otherwise! The bon vivant type of parson died out, and in the course of time was supplanted by one who was so imbued with the reverential attitude that he introduced the "deep note" into the most trivial conversation, and spoke, moved, and behaved as if he were officiating at the altar instead of at a tea party. There was also a noticeable difference in the behaviour of people in church and in their attitude towards their clergy. Whereas it had been quite customary to go to sleep in order somehow to pass the time during Divine Service, it came to be considered irreverent, and, therefore, not "good form." As to the parson, he was no longer merely regarded as a "good fellow" paid to preach sermons and keep an eye on the souls of his flock, but was looked up to and venerated as a superior being. In the eighteenth century he may have been, and no doubt often *was,* loved by his congregation; in the nineteenth century he was *revered* by them. And they were as unconscious of the fact that the typical Victorian clergyman was a prig as their grandfathers had been unconscious of the fact that the parson of *their* day was a religious anomaly, and as Handel himself, when he wrote it, was unconscious that his music would ever engender priggishness. Although it is related of him that he composed some of his arias with tears running down his cheeks, it is also related of him that he was addicted to swearing upon most occasions, that he was a practical and shrewd man of business, enjoyed good food, aristocratic society, and was distinctly ambitious—in short—he was *not* a prig. The irony, however, that he should unwittingly and eventually induce priggishness in others is only surpassed by an even greater one for which the influence of his music was in no small measure responsible. We allude to the veto set by many clergymen and laymen upon oratorio itself, the grounds being that it was *irreverent*. According to Dean Ramsey, who opposed this strange notion.

> It is well known that objections have been made to the performance of oratorios and the attendance on such performances. Indeed, they have been considered in some sort profane or sacrilegious; and well-meaning, conscientious persons have felt it their duty to protest against oratorios, forbidding their families to attend on such performances, as they would forbid their attendance on scenes of mere earthly gaiety, on the opera, and on theatrical entertainments.[4]

It may seem extravagant to speak of reverence run riot, yet not only does the foregoing warrant that phrase, but much else in the Victorian age warrants it also. Now reverence and the idea of sacredness are, of course, very closely allied, but it so happens that an exaggerated idea of sacredness gives rise to an equally exaggerated idea of unsacredness: it is this latter idea, which caused many of the Victorians to regard all worldly pleasures, so-called, as sinful. The theatre, the opera, were regarded as unsacred—therefore, to derive enjoyment from them was "to indulge in an enthusiasm which leads astray—which leads to the tasting of a pleasure, which is of the forbidden tree . . ." as one might paraphrase the article in the *Quarterly Review* already quoted. Nor can we fail to trace the same cause at the back of all prudery, especially in matters of sex: prudery being nothing more than the result of a perverted sense of reverence. Though sex was a necessary, if enjoyable, evil, it was, the Victorians imagined, not officially countenanced by God, and hence all reference to it in print and in mixed society was prohibited. Ideas associated with "respect for the ladies"—another phase of reverence—also played a part, for it was an "ungentlemanly" act for a man to discuss matters of sex with a married woman, even though her innocence could hardly be jeopardized thereby, as it was for him to discuss them with an unmarried one. The concomitants and variants of all this are well known; the Bowdlerization of the classics became a popular device, though no one thought of Bowdlerizing the Bible; classical statuary was fitted with fig leaves; synonyms were employed to veil the supposed impropriety of certain words; sudden excursions into Latin were customary in scientific books; it is unnecessary to elaborate further.

But even turning from the more delicate relations of life to the more practical, we find again how many of them were associated with reverence in the broadest sense of the word. When women considered that certain occupations and certain pastimes were *infra dig.,* it was because they exaggeratedly revered themselves and their own sex, while the opposite sex aided and abetted them in this. All concern on the part of people for their own dignity or that of others is always inspired by this sense of reverence. Indeed, only in an age when it so forcibly predominated would it have been possible for even a queen to say to her minister who was practically dying: "I am sorry I cannot ask you to sit down. . . ."

There was yet another by-product of reverence, or the sense of sacredness conjoined with dignity, which was a most marked characteristic of the Victorian outlook; it was the glorification of duty as an incentive to action. To do this, that, or the other for its own sake, or because one wished to do it, was not sufficient; such reasons, in fact, were far too frivolous, too undignified to be countenanced; but if actions could somehow be exalted by a nimbus of moral obligation, thus denuding them of every vestige of association with pleasure, then the Victorian's mind was at peace, and his self-respect gratified. Thus arose the idea of the sacredness of duty.

With all his gifts, Handel was not a revolutionist like Wagner; he was more of the Tchaikovsky type of composer who elaborated the existing musical devices of his day and combined them with a wealth of melodic exuberance. In the case of Tchaikovsky those devices or conventions were connected with the sonata form, in the case of Handel they were connected with fugal writing, and, as already said, with sequences and reiterations (i.e., conventions) in themselves. Why these latter, by the law of correspondences, should have induced formalism in life, we need not repeat. Yet the law of correspondences does not end here; just because, owing to his technique, Handel's beauty and grandeur were formal and unsubtle, so were the beauty and grandeur of the Victorian epoch . . . with its false Gothic architecture, its massive mahogany furniture in the dining room, its enormous walnut or mahogany beds and wardrobes in the bedroom, its red plush chairs with gilt frames in the drawing room, its wax flowers and gaudy-feathered stuffed birds under glass cases, its Crystal Palace, its Albert Memorial, and many other objects depictive of formalism too numerous to mention.

Yet all this was only one aspect of the Handelian influence—the other and earlier one was manifested in a predilection for the sombre, for black horsehair sofas and chairs, for exaggerated widows' weeds. And why? Because in certain temperaments the awe and reverence engendered by Handel's music inspired the love of the funereal, the hyper-serious; in fact, a false idea of the spiritual.

A measure of Handel's glory had spread—soon after his death— to Germany, but not so to Austria, and still less to France. Indeed, as Romain Rolland writes: "We" (of France) "still await the full revelation of this great luminous tragic art, so akin to the aims of ancient Greece."[5]

And how significant is this admission! In the eighteenth century the English were temperamentally in several respects closer akin to the French than they have ever been since; after the advent of Handel they became widely divergent. It was quite customary for the Victorians to deplore the frivolity, the outspokenness, the moral laxity, the worldliness, the Sabbath-breaking habits of "those people on the continent," quite forgetting that not so many years back similar conditions had obtained in England. It is true that Germany was also included in this sweeping opprobrium, because its theatres and some of its shops were open on Sundays; yet the habits of the German people, far from being frivolous, were very much the opposite. They were preeminently a serious nation who loved serious literature, serious art, and serious music; they were also a conventional people. These national traits were partly due to Handel, but even more to the influence of Johann Sebastian Bach, as we shall show in the next chapter. With regard to the Austrians, they retained the national gaiety and *joie de vivre*, which are also characteristic of the French; and it is an interesting fact that they derived much of their musical nourishment from Mozart, whom even today they worship almost as a demi-god. This does not imply, however, that the works of Handel were and are never performed in Austria, but that the Austrians were late to recognize his genius and that in their country he does not occupy, and never *has* occupied, the place of glory allotted to him in England. In Italy also he has by no means become a national institution, and here, despite so much professional religiosity, there is, in consequence, very little reverence. This fact was noticeable to no less a person than Mendelssohn, who wrote in 1830:

> The Italians have a religion, but do not believe in it; they have a
> Pope and a government, but they turn them into ridicule; they can
> recall a brilliant and heroic past, but they do not value it. . . . It is
> really quite revolting to see their unconcern about the death of the
> Pope, and their unseemly merriment during the ceremonies. I myself
> saw the corpse lying in state, and the priests standing round inces-
> santly whispering and laughing.

But then a nation with such a passion for the ultra-melodious will always be too gay-hearted to be reverent.

8
Comparison between the Influence of Handel and Bach

With the death of Johann Sebastian Bach in 1750—just nine years before that of Handel—the greatest polyphonist the world has ever known passed out of the musical arena. Indeed, to him, as Schumann wrote, "Music owes almost as great a debt as a religion owes to its founder." Yet Bach was more than the greatest of polyphonists: he was an inventor of rare melodic beauty and a harmonist of remarkable daring. It is therefore small wonder that he has been termed "the father of the whole of our modern music," and that his name is the symbol of

the completion and perfection of Christian tonal art during the Middle Ages and the Reformation. He is even credited with the entire enfranchisement of music, for by his creativeness in the field of purely instrumental composition the final, full and complete impress of liberty was forever set to the tonal art. . . .

Now could it give utterance in precise, intelligible tones to the innermost feelings. . . . No longer did it require the support of poetry, biblical, or liturgical texts, church services, civic ceremonies, or dramatic representation to assist it in making itself understood.

It was supreme in its own realm of independent tone, sole sovereign in its world of instrumental music. From a dependent vassal Bach elevated it into the proud position of a queen, responsible to herself alone.[1]

Such are the eulogistic rhapsodies of the historian we shall several times quote in this book. The writer in *Grove's Dictionary* expresses himself in an equally eulogistic if less flowery manner. Bach he maintains

created an entirely new vocal style based on instrumental principles, carried it to the summit of perfection, and there left it. . . . Though his masterly counterpoint is generally spoken of as the special mark of his genius . . . his real power lies less in the almost inconceivable facility and dexterity with which he manages the complicated network of parts than in that formal conformation of the movements, which resulted from his manner of writing; in this he exhibits a consistency, fertility and feeling for organic completeness, which are truly inimitable. His melody, his harmony, and his periods all seem of one mould, *an indestructible spirit of severe logic and unalterable conformity to law pervades the whole as well as the parts.* This wonderful unity of idea and formal construction gives the stamp of the true work of art to Bach's compositions, and explains the magical attraction which they exert on those who make them their earnest study. [Italics are mine.]

The above requires but little elucidation; it shows us that the keynote of Bach's genius was *profundity,* yet not an arid profundity: dull, unattractive, fit only for the entertainment of technicians, but one replete with high inspiration and inventiveness. Bach, in fact, was not merely a composer; he was, in one sense, also a mathematician. Only the latter could have brought counterpoint to such a state of perfection. Somewhat similar to a chess-player, he had an extraordinary aptitude for thinking out combinations, and although through his consummate skill he never allowed the workmanship to become undesirably apparent, painstaking must have been a pronounced feature of his modus operandi. It would be difficult to imagine that Bach could "dash off" a whole oratorio in three weeks, as Handel is said to have done; for Bach's "general predilection for dissonance, crossing of parts and suspensions" naturally led to a more complicated style of writing, and one which demanded considerable mental effort. Whereas "Handel is somewhat lax and easy going in his treatment of art forms, Bach is always strict and pointed,"[2] with the result that less intelligence is required to grasp the former's compositions than those of the latter;[3] less intellect—considerably so—was also required in the writing of them.

But to examine the effects of Bach's music, as will be evident to all those who have obtained some insight into the principal argument of this book, they exercised a most marked influence upon the *mentality*. The mathematical ingenuity of his fuguewriting alone contributed greatly to this influence. It also with its "imitations" and *stretto* effects made possible an easier "give-and-take" in the realm of the mental;* or, better phrased, facilitated the exchange and assimilation of ideas: for what else constitutes a fugue but the exchange of one or more *musical* ideas between moving parts? From the day when Bach's music spread abroad date the vastly increased intellectuality of the German people and the endeavours of some of their greatest thinkers: his music was likewise responsible for the rich harvest of subsequent German composers. The reason why Germany and not England was so prolific in this respect is to be found in Bach's influence in contradistinction to that of Handel. However necessary and beneficial in many ways the effects of Handel's work may have been, they were hostile to original thinking and to the production of *creative* musicians; and it is owing to this that after Purcell, England entered upon the most colourless period of its musical history. Because Handel among other things indirectly inspired conventionalism, the English composers after his time were conventional and mediocre; they entertained too much reverence for tradition, and hence were imitators, not creators; only when his influence abated

*See effects of *Canon*, chapter 29.

and was counteracted by others did English music once more revive.

But this does not imply that Bach's music inspired no reverence: it did; but a different type of reverence: a more mental, a more reasoning, and consequently a less purely emotional type. The *Ehrfurcht* of the Germans is directed towards the achievements of great men, towards profound art, toward the grandeur of nature—it manifests itself in a different form from that which we have studied in connection with England; it is more philosophical and less religiously conventional. Indeed, Bach with his musical logic aroused a remarkable taste for philosophy in the Teutonic people. Even some sixty years ago when his influence had already been much mingled with that of others, while the youths and men of England preferred to gossip about cricket, football, or golf, the German youths were earnestly preoccupied with the "why, whence, and whither" of human existence. Although, as we have indicated in our last chapter, the nineteenth century in England was a preeminently serious one, that seriousness was more puritanical than intellectual; there was a degree of unconscious hypocrisy in many of its features. Pietistic books, for instance, were disseminated in place of literature of high artistic worth, and even the daring and unorthodox George Eliot could not refrain from liberally tincturing her novels with what Nietzsche caustically terms "moralic acid"—hence a large proportion of her fame. Nevertheless, because she lived with a man who was not her husband, it was considered "shocking" to read her works; and many are the instances of people who slipped them under a cushion when surprised by the appearance of a visitor. . . .

We have examined the general effects of Bach's monumental genius, and we may now turn to those connected with his smaller and less profound works. Although the elements, which went to the making of these, were slightly less sequential and repetitious than those employed by Handel, they tended to produce a certain amount of formal thinking. In some minds this was distinctly beneficial, for it brought about law and order in the mentality, but in others it tended to produce "strait-lacedness," a quality that was greatly augmented when they came under the influence of Handel. The net result of this may be seen in a species of intellectual conventionality, a ponderousness for which the Germans at one time were notorious. Co-existent with this ponderousness there were signs of another type of conventionality, that which is best summed up in the one expressive adjective, *kleinstädtisch.** It was a characteristic of nineteenth-century German life, which more than any other resembled Victorianism, and it was in some measure due to a very curious fact connected with the post-mortem fame of Bach himself. For exactly one hundred years his more profound and harmonically inventive works were laid aside, and in the interim, or, rather, a part of it, those of Handel took precedence in Germany and shed their influence upon the German people. Had Bach's greater works, such as *St. Matthew's Passion* and *St. John's Passion,* held full sway from the time of their production, the nineteenth century in the "Fatherland" would have been less kleinstädtisch than it was. And this, owing to the dissonances that were prominent factors in both these works. For dissonance has a marked effect on the mental organism, as we will explain in a subsequent chapter; it renders it more flexible, and so makes the thinker less conventionally minded. But in consequence of the temporary withdrawal of Bach's more discordant influences and the predominance of Handel's, not only did the kleinstädtisch element thrive, but there also came into being that extraordinary genus of people, termed *Kulturphilister.†* Bach had first intellectualised the Germans, then Handel appeared and conventionalised them, and the Kulturphilister were one of the curious by-products of the composite music. They cannot quite accurately be termed intellectual snobs—though there is a flavour of snobbishness about some of them—they are mainly people whose philistinism is connected with things intellectual instead of things crude and inartistic.

We have pointed out that Bach's larger works were laid aside for a hundred years, and it is known to most music-lovers that to Mendelssohn we owe their resuscitation in 1829, when the *Matthew Passion* was re-performed in Berlin. After this event "a powerful excitement seized the

*"Small-townish." Inadequately rendered "provincial."
†culture-philistines

musical world; (in Germany) people began to feel that an infinite depth and fullness of originality united with a consummate power of formal construction was lying hidden in these neglected works. Performances of the Passion and of other vocal music of Bach took place in Berlin and elsewhere"[4]; in fact, his music was diffused all over the "Fatherland."

But although its intellectualizing influence—which even now is still operative—was thus diffused, it was, and is, mingled with so many other influences that it is difficult to gauge the exact nature and extent of its effect. Suffice it to say that intellectuality in Germany is more general than in almost any other European country, and that its conventions and intellectual philistinism are fast disappearing. With regard to England, although some of Bach's smaller works gained a hearing—notably the organ fugues—around 1840, the *Matthew Passion*, in its entirety, was not performed until 1854, just 125 years after its original production in Germany. Thus, the field of oratorio was held almost entirely by Handel until 1846, when Mendelssohn presented his *Elijah* to the English public. Had Johann Sebastian Bach appeared earlier on the scene, with the full array of his very daring* harmonies and his masterly counterpoint, we emphatically believe that the characteristics of the Victorian era would have been, if not entirely different, at any rate greatly modified. Intellectual rather than merely pietistic seriousness would have been more general; religion would not have become so stereotyped, for people would have thought along more independent lines instead of being content to imitate the thoughts of others. As it was, Handel's "simple grandeur," his completely euphonious harmonies, were not of a nature calculated either to increase the mentality or to modify its conventional tendencies; this was left for Bach and other musicians to accomplish at a later date.

---

*Daring for the period in which they were written.

9

Beethoven, Sympathy and Psychoanalysis

Just twenty years after Bach—modest, indigent, yet content with the obscure position he occupied—had passed away, a soul of a very different nature made its appearance in the little town of Bonn on the Rhine. It already speaks for the vagaries of his character—we allude to Ludwig van Beethoven—that he firmly believed he was born two years later than he actually *was*. Moreover, he could not be convinced when confronted, in the prime of life, with a copy of his certificate of baptism. "This seems not correct," he wrote on the back of it, "there was a Ludwig before me." Precisely, but it was a female child named Ludwig Maria; and even then she was born not two, but three years prior to Beethoven. Yet, considering the particular work for which he was destined, it is, if anything, strange that his temperament should not have exhibited even greater peculiarities.

The prefix *van* has led some people to suppose that he was of aristocratic descent, but in Dutch that word is not a sign of nobility, and must not be confounded with the French *de* or the German *von*. His mother was the daughter of a *chef*, his father, a man of irascible temper and irregular habits, a vocalist in the chapel of Clement Augustus, the Elector of Cologne. It is more than probable that the son may have inherited some of the father's temper but, on the other hand, he must also have inherited many of the qualities of his mother, who is described as a woman of soft heart and easy ways, inspiring much love in her afterward-to-be-famous son. Indeed, it is just this strange admixture of the intensely lovable and the hot-tempered, tactless and ill-mannered in Beethoven's character that has proved so puzzling to benevolent biographers and so disappointing to numerous hero-worshippers.

Yet there are deeper reasons underlying all these characteristics—deeper than the impress of humble breeding, deeper even than the results of those syphilitic affections,[1] which manifested themselves at an early period of his life. *If Beethoven's character had been otherwise*[2] it is not conceivable that he could have discharged his singular mission, *which was to portray in sound every variety of human emotion.* As Bach had been the greatest polyphonist hitherto known, Beethoven was the greatest musical psychologist. For this reason it was essential that he should be born to suffer, born with manifold difficulties against which to contend; difficulties of temperament, of external circumstances, and of corporeal difficulties. In order to express the entire gamut of human emotions in the cipher of music, he had first to experience, if not all, at any rate most of them; the rest was achieved through the imagination. But that very imagination set his emotional organism in a whirl of conflicting forces; it resembled the body of a medium who allows herself to be controlled by every variety of spirit. Small wonder that his mind has been compared to his own journal—a medley "of the most passionate and personal reflections, prayers, aspirations, complaints, memoranda of expenses and household matters, notes about his music, rules for conduct, quotations from books,"[3] and what not.

We have sought to explain the connection between the life and character of this remarkable man, and his equally remarkable mission; yet, even so, we have only described that mission in part and have not dealt with its full significance. For it may be asked: "What is the value of portraying every species of human emotion, especially the lower ones, in musical cipher, is this not merely to degrade music, to render material the most immaterial of all the arts?" And the question is a perfectly legitimate one, and may even, in some cases, voice that rather enigmatical dislike, which a number of people at the present time feel towards Beethoven's work. The value of a thing must, however, to a large extent be judged by its effects, as we need hardly point out, and it is with these we are concerned in this book, and not with questions of artistic dogma.

The influence of Beethoven's music, then, may be placed under two headings: (1) it induced Sympathy on a scale hitherto unknown; (2) it made possible the introduction later on of the science of Psychoanalysis to a baffled and horrified public; it was, in fact, the forerunner of this therapeutic science.

To deal first with the sympathy-inducing aspect of Beethoven's work: the depictive value of music over and above that of literature, drama, painting and poetry, consists in its total lack of restrictedness, and in its direct appeal to the intuition or the subconscious. As implied in chapter 1, people intuitively or subconsciously assimilate the meaning of music without—though there are countless exceptions—being objectively aware of the fact. Thus, the great advantage of tone-poetry is that it can express anything and *everything* in a cipher, which the heart understands, without the interference of the conscious mind. As most people must realize, it is, with literature, the word that shocks and the mind that is shocked; and the tendency being to turn from all that is "unpleasant," luxurious humanity, in accordance with the old adage relative to ignorance, wisdom, and bliss, closes the shutters upon vast fields of knowledge. But that is the very procedure, which is utterly hostile to the development of true sympathy; for, hackneyed as the phrase may be, it is nonetheless a fact that only when we understand all can we forgive all. It therefore became necessary that a medium of expression should be given to the world, which compelled people to acquire that understanding, whether they wished to do so or not. This medium was Beethoven's music, for it caused them to realize not only the more obvious troubles of others: grief, deprivation, sickness, yearning, but also—in themselves as well as in others—that vast array of strange emotions, feelings, passions, of which men were too ashamed to speak. It was, no doubt, an instinctive recognition of this compelling force in Beethoven's message, which caused one of his symphonies to be termed *ein sittenverderbendes Werk.**

In our review of the Victorian era and its characteristics, no mention was made of sympathy. The truth is that although there were philanthropists—when have there not been?—the power to feel *with*, and not merely to feel *for*, was lacking. An excess of reverence and especially of conventionality proved hostile to this "gentle art," and, consequently, we find that so many pious people in that era were, despite their creed, surprisingly intolerant and unsympathetic. They were so concerned with their feelings towards God that they had little or nothing left over for their fellow man. Such sympathy as did exist was regulated by convention as much as conduct, thought and habit were so regulated. There were some things about which it was considered wrong to feel sympathetic; a woman, for example, who "went astray," no matter how much she suffered in consequence, was emphatically no fit subject for compassion, and much the same attitude was adopted towards miscreants and criminals of all descriptions.

Nevertheless, since the appearance of Beethoven a prodigious variety of changes have taken and *are* taking place. Music and other educative influences are permitted in prisons, books have been written contending that criminality is a form of insanity and not merely the lust to do evil, and capital punishment is engendering more and more opponents. Close friendships between members of opposite sexes no longer provoke scandals. The attitude of children towards their parents is no longer one of mere dutifulness and exaggerated respect, but is one more closely resembling friendship and mutual understanding. Furthermore, it was the tolerance-inspiring effect of Beethoven's music, which gave rise to the writings of Havelock Ellis, Forel, Krafft-Ebing, Bloch, and others—those painstaking and self-sacrificing investigators of sexual psychology. As the alienist attempted to show that the misdeeds of the criminal were not always actuated by the lust to do evil, so did these

---

Grove has translated this "a dangerously immoral composition" there being no exact equivalent in English. It means, however, even more: "a work which spells ruin to morals."

writers attempt to show that the misdemeanors of sexual inverts and perverts were not actuated by sheer love of vice. The vast increase of charitable organizations, having sympathy as their raison d'être, is also to be attributed to Beethoven's influence. In fine, his music helped to bring about that greater unity between the heart and the mind, which is the prerequisite of true understanding: it humanized humanity.

We may now pass on to the more specifically psychological aspects of our subject.

Czerny has written relative to Beethoven and his improvisations that "in whatever company he might chance to be, he knew how to produce such an effect upon every hearer that frequently not an eye remained dry, while many persons would break out into loud sobs; for there was something wonderful in his expression, in addition to the beauty and originality of his ideas . . ." Not that Beethoven himself wished to produce this rather embarrassing effect, since he would often indignantly exclaim: "We artists don't want tears, we want applause." But there existed in his music an element, which seemed irresistibly to bring to the surface suppressed emotions that could only find vent in weeping. And although personal magnetism may have enhanced this element to a certain degree, long after Beethoven himself had passed from this earth-plane, people who listened to, but more especially *played,* his works were conscious of a pronounced emotional relief. His music gave utterance to all those feelings, which they could not, perhaps even dared not, express in any other way.

It is a well-known fact that to express a sorrow, which gnaws at the heart—whether it be to a friend in the shape of a confidence, to a priest before the confessional, or on paper in the form of verse—is to disburden oneself and so lighten the soul. On the other hand, to repress that sorrow is to endanger both health and sanity. For this reason the wise physician encourages those who have sustained some great shock, or are suffering from some inexplicable fear or desire, to talk about it freely.

Now the Victorian age, with its prudishness and proprieties, was an age of repressions, and the emotions, which ought to have found an outlet, were forced *inwards,* with results exceedingly detrimental to the nervous system. This was particularly marked in the case of unmarried women, for not only was it considered *wrong* for them to feel anything in the nature of sexual emotions, but, as strenuous exercise in the form of hockey, tennis, and other games was tabooed, no corrective to these emotions was available. It is not surprising, therefore, that the early-Victorian women "dissolved into tears," had "the vapours," or fainted on the slightest provocation. It must also be remembered that they were considered old and unattractive, hence ineligible, after they had passed their thirtieth year, so that the number of unsatisfied women was very considerable. Indeed, the consequences to the national health would have been disastrous had it not been for Beethoven's music. When women played his sonatas, expressive of a host of turbulent emotions, of violent passions, and unabashed yearnings, they were actually giving vent to their feelings, and thus liberating what otherwise would have remained encaged. And it was more than mere sexual passions, which they were able to liberate in this way, for Beethoven, being so profound a musical psychologist, expressed those less natural and more reprehensible emotions—hatred, jealousy, and all their variants; he also expressed intense remorse, despair, and the abyss of gloom. Nor was this all; by the plummet of his music he fathomed and set free a vast number of emotions, which had been forgotten and had sunk into the subconscious, there to make their ravages upon the health of their generators. It is this searching power in Beethoven's work, which prompted us to write that he was the forerunner of psychoanalysis—he *was* in one sense a psychoanalyst, and this is why, as his music became more widely diffused, and the Victorian age progressed, its women gradually became less hysterical and less subject to fainting and tearfulness.

There may be some, however, who will question the psychoanalytical power in Beethoven's music; yet the fact remains that its effect on a large number of people is to induce those taletelling reveries, which reveal the content of the subconscious mind, in a manner nothing else *can*. In these reveries may be found mysterious gratification of secret longings; in imaginary scene after scene, and situation after situation, the dreamers visualise themselves as hero or heroine of their own innermost desire-drama; natures forced by circumstances into the hypocrisy of repression become, during such moments, their true selves; unsatisfied cravings, no matter how fantastic, are assuaged; the frustrations, the thwartings of daily life are forgotten; impossible-seeming ideals are achieved; even the god-like instinct to create, which slumbers in the heart of every human being, may be stirred, just as may old submerged rancours and resentments, and the lust to destroy. The subconscious prisoner is freed alike from the gaolership of social customs, and from that of the conscious mind itself. The action of that conscious mind, indeed, is, in the majority of people, temporarily suspended during the process of listening to music; it is, in fact, lulled into a species of quiescence, instead of being definitely concentrated upon the sounds played. Those sounds, of course, are heard by the ear, but more than as an actual focusing—point for the conscious attention they serve as a stimulus to set the thoughts wandering and to allow the subconscious—as in the dream-state—to have full sway.

It is safe to say that a good many types of music tend to produce this "releasing" effect upon the subconscious, but not one to such an extent as that of Beethoven, for he alone among musicians knew how to express just those secrets of the inner mind, and, expressing them, to awaken countless echoes in the minds of his hearers.

So far we have only dealt with the more passionate element in Beethoven's music, and nothing has been said about his extraordinary fund of humour, which plays a very significant role, in many of his compositions. It is a striking fact that as his deafness became more pronounced, so did his humour; when he realized that his terrible affliction might be incurable, he wrote some of the most hilariously abandoned of all his works. But his humour was not like that of Mendelssohn, sprightly, happy, fairy-like; it was the humor of the gallows; the sardonic laughter of a man who has lost *all!* The last movement of the Seventh Symphony, the last movement of the Eighth, and the Scherzo of the Ninth, are all—especially the latter—examples of this *Galgenhumor.* And this was not manifested alone in his works, but also in his life; it was at this particular period of his career that he developed an embarrassing taste for horseplay, in and out of season. That it often caused offence there are many anecdotes to prove, but it often aroused sympathy as well, for it was the jocularity of despair. Before his mission was complete Beethoven was destined to feel even *this,* that he might portray it in his music, and so make others *understand.* No ordinary humour could have achieved such a result, because ordinary humour does not awaken sympathy, it awakens only laughter; but the humour of the gallows is more poignant even than straightforward pathos, hence it makes a far more powerful appeal. True, there are those who may hear the three movements above-mentioned without being objectively conscious of their real meaning, but the inner being is affected and understands, and that is all that matters.

When the first monument was erected to Beethoven, the orator on that occasion said: "No mourning wife, no son, no daughter wept at his grave, but a world wept at it." Yet even the "world" did not then understand the complete debt of gratitude they owed to him whose loss they so bitterly mourned. Nor could they understand, for it was another generation who was to reap the full harvest of Beethoven's genius. Those who followed him to the grave had experienced the most complete ecstasy through his music, but not its more momentous results. It is the prostitute and the foundling, the incurable and the very aged—those who have perhaps never even heard his name—who in reality owe him most of all.

10 *The Mendelssohnian Sympathy*

There could hardly have existed two more diametrically opposed characters than those of Mendelssohn and Beethoven; and yet strangely enough the two men were, however unconsciously, working to the same end: the instilment of Sympathy into the human soul. But their methods were as divergent as their characters; Beethoven, metaphorically speaking, showed one side of the picture, Mendelssohn the other.

It is instructive to observe how widely Mendelssohn's life differed from his predecessor's, not only at the beginning, but practically throughout; how he was to be surrounded by an atmosphere of sympathy from his earliest years. His home circle, in fact, was the very antithesis of Beethoven's; instead of a drunken father shedding worries and miseries all around him, Mendelssohn's father "was a man of firm character and great general ability; and though not an artist, was gifted with far keener insight than most *dilettanti* in the higher qualities of art."[1] Nor was Mendelssohn less fortunate as regards his mother, who, in addition to her capabilities as an excellent but gentle disciplinarian, possessed many and varied accomplishments. "She spoke French, English, and Italian fluently, was a good Greek scholar . . . played and sang with taste and judgment, and drew beautifully."[2] But above all else, she appears, according to Hiller, to have manifested that "infinite kindness and gentleness," that loving interest in people and their doings, which can be summed up in the one word: sympathy.

In his biography on Mendelssohn, Dr. Hiller wrote:

> Gifts of genius were in him united to the most careful culture, tenderness of heart to sharpness of understanding, playful facility in everything that he attempted to powerful energy for the highest tasks. A noble feeling of gratitude penetrated his pure heart at every good thing that fell to his lot. This pious disposition, pious in the best sense of the word, was the secret of his constant readiness to give pleasure and to show active sympathy.[3]

And it was just the foregoing combination of elements in Mendelssohn's character, translated into music, which made so direct and instantaneous an appeal. The gentle sweetness of so many of his melodies, combined with the happy but never boisterous elements in his more vivacious passages, could not fail to affect mankind—it brought home to them the beauty of sympathy in itself. No music prior to Mendelssohn's had insistently breathed such exquisite tenderness; there had been rare moments in Beethoven,* but they were fleeting, and all too soon to be swept away by the more violent winds of passion; but Mendelssohn breathed sweetness throughout, even when gay and vivacious. He had learned to value it from the earliest years of his life; he had seen it in his family circle, and through his music he carried it into those of others. After hearing one of his melodies, people felt soothed and softened, and consequently more tender and sympathetic towards all those in their immediate environment: their wives, their children, their sisters, their brothers. It was impossible to resist the dulcet compassion of such strains as "O Rest in the Lord," or the melody in the second movement of the violin concerto. Yet this was not all; the aching soul was not only comforted, but cheered by his fairy-like gaiety. Not as with Beethoven's music were people stirred up into a state of intense emotionality, but lulled into a

---

*In his violin concerto, for example.

condition of peace or tranquil felicity. Mendelssohn's music radiated a serene happiness; he was the musical analogy of Florence Nightingale, not as she really was, but "as facile fancy painted her. . . ." Yet his modesty was such that it seems he was unconscious of the power in his work, even though he experienced that deep sympathy of which it was an expression. For when writing to a friend in distress, he says: "Have I also not felt from the bottom of my heart how at such moments all art and poetry and everything else that is dear and precious to us seem so empty and comfortless, so hateful and paltry, and the only thought that does one any good is 'Oh, that God would help!'"*

Still, though he felt thus for the sorrows of his fellows, it was never his mission to portray those sorrows in music as Beethoven had done; it was for him to supply what the former had lacked. Beethoven's great art was to awaken compassion by, as it were, portraying the wretched and the destitute in all their misery; Mendelssohn's was to achieve the same result by portraying them made happy; as we have said, he showed the reverse side of the picture. There were many to whom the tragic grandiosities of Beethoven's works were repellent; they proved in those days almost too soul-stirring, and some objected to being thus inconveniently stirred; they chafed at being made to feel the numberless tragedies of life. To those people the soothing sweetness of Mendelssohn especially appealed, and although they were not objectively aware of it, a sympathy was awakened in the heart, which made them desire happiness for their fellows.

As we know, there is a type of emotional epicureanism, which prompts some persons only to allow themselves to taste of those feelings that are pleasurable. "I want to hear nothing that is unpleasant," they say, "therefore, don't tell me about it."

These people are selfish and lacking in sympathy. Yet there are others who, although they dread the spectacle of suffering and go out of their way to avoid it, nevertheless work toward its amelioration; they wish that everyone should be happy, because they see the great

---

*Letter to Ferdinand Hiller.

desirability of happiness, because by nature they are inherently sympathetic. And it was just this perception of the desirability of a more diffused happiness that Mendelssohn aroused and strengthened by the gayer aspects of his art.

There are not a few who detect a certain melancholy in some of Mendelssohn's work, yet if they look closer they must realize that it is not the melancholy of sorrow, but the rather pleasant melancholy of the poet who now and then enjoys the luxury of feeling sad. In Mendelssohn it was largely inspired by the artistic necessity of contrast. His nature was not such that—like Beethoven—the more wretched, the more agitated he felt, the more did he compose; under the stress of worry and genuine grief, the delicate flower of his organism withered and lost all its strength. The exigencies of fame—which, by the way, he never sought—combined with the annoyances of petty jealousies, began to tell upon his health, which was finally to be shattered beyond repair by the death of the sister he cared for so much.

It was in 1847 that he died, but already a year previously his powers, it would seem, had begun to wane. A child of sympathy who loved the bright and the beautiful, he was no stoic; and with all his admiration for Goethe, whom he had known in his youth, he was not a philosopher. Everything came easy to him except fortitude. . . . Yet, perhaps if he had not known how to suffer in excess himself, he would have felt less for the sufferings of others, and could never have tinctured his music with that sweetness, which was to show the beauty and dulcitude of sympathy itself. Thus, the world would have lost the one being who above all else was the tone-poet of compassion, of tenderness, and fraternal love.

The immense popularity, which Mendelssohn enjoyed, especially in England during his lifetime, was only to be increased after his death. That he enhanced the sympathy-arousing effects of Beethoven's music is obvious from the even greater increase of charitable institutions, which became manifest some twenty years after Mendelssohn had passed away.

Between the years 1879 and 1904, no fewer than fifty-eight charities were inaugurated in London alone. Sympathy for the blind, for the deaf and dumb, for the dangers and discomforts of maternity, for the illegitimate child, for those suffering from venereal diseases, had been enormously augmented. And it is not only the welfare of the needy that has been considered, but also that of the ordinary citizen. Apart from the significant fact that the Anti-Sweating League was formed in 1889, public parks, libraries, recreation grounds, and so forth in astonishing profusion have come into existence. Mendelssohn sowed the first seeds in the heart of man, which were to blossom into the exalted ideal of "well-being for all."

II
Frédéric Chopin, the Apostle of Refinement

Chopin was born not only in the same year as Felix Mendelssohn, but in the same month—February, 1809—and that there was a certain similarity of temperament between the two composers, though their influence on humanity was destined to be different, speaks much for the truth of astrology.

Several biographers have painted the boy Chopin as a "moonstruck, pale, sentimental" creature, with no stamina and no joie de vivre; but then biographers, like portrait-painters, are not overly incommoded by a sense of accuracy. It was quite enough that Chopin in childhood should burst into tears whenever he heard music, for them to draw these erroneous conclusions, as it was enough that some thirty-eight years later he should desire to be buried in his dress-clothes, for Lombroso to pronounce him a lunatic. Yet, unfortunately for this learned scientist's diagnosis, Chopin never expressed any such desire.[1]

Nor did he abandon "the woman whom he tenderly loved, because she offered a chair to someone else before giving the same invitation to himself." For here, as Huneker points out, "we have merely a George Sand story raised to the dignity of a diagnosed symptom. It is like the other nonsense," he contemptuously adds.[2]

The fact is that although there was hardly a thing relative to Chopin about which any two persons could agree, they were at least unanimous that he lived in Paris, where untruthful gossiping—at any rate in the nineteenth century—was reduced to an art, if hardly to a fine one. All the same, from among the tares of pseudo-romantic untruths, which sprang up around his enigmatical personality, we are able to glean that as a boy he was neither robust nor very delicate, that he was intelligent, vivacious, sensitive, with a merry disposition, and a fondness for practical jokes. Like Mendelssohn, he was brought up in an atmosphere of "love and refinement," both his parents being well bred and unusually cultivated. His Polish mother, born of poor but noble stock, appears to have been an ideal mother, his father an agreeable Frenchman with a scholarly turn of mind; as for his sisters, "they were gifted, gentle, and disposed to pet him. . . ."[3] Though the Chopin family was never affluent, they lived in easy circumstances, and ample money was forthcoming to pay for Frédéric's musical education; the supposition, therefore, that he was born to poverty and early suffering is one of those pseudo-romantic fables, which have no foundation in fact. There are, however, reasons for supposing that at the age of seventeen he outgrew his strength, having first overtaxed it with his studies at the Lyceum; but the result does not appear to have been very serious, for Karasowski informs us that he reached manhood without ever having suffered from any complaint more alarming than a cold. It is true that his mother and sisters were constantly admonishing him "to wrap up carefully in cold weather,"[4] and this rather exaggerated solicitude might possess a certain significance, did it not happen to be almost a universal trait in continental mothers and sisters, even when the object of their solicitude is comparatively robust. Other evidence set forth to prove that Chopin was a very delicate youth is hardly more convincing. Thus, we are told, for one thing, that "he was no friend of long excursions on foot, and preferred to lie down and dream under beautiful trees," and, for another, that he "objected to smoking."[5] But then "poets," as a rule, are given to dreaming and prefer to use their brains rather than their legs; as for smoking, there are countless nonsmokers who enjoy excellent health.

Even the verdict upon Chopin, pronounced in 1830 by the music-lovers of Warsaw when he was twenty-one, must be taken *cum grano salis,* namely, that because he looked thin and pale, he would, like so many geniuses, die young: for it is obvious that these romantic pessimists were hypnotized by a facile catchphrase, which was hardly consistent with fact. If they were thinking of *musical* geniuses, then the "so many" were reducible to Mozart and Schubert, seeing that Palestrina, both the Scarlattis, Handel, and Bach, all lived to be old men. Nor did Chopin die so very young after all—he was in his fortieth year when he breathed his last, and for Early Victorian conceptions that was middle age.

Nevertheless, we do not seek to prove that Chopin was the embodiment of health and strength—far from it—but merely to dispel the notion that from his cradle to his grave he was a "morose and melancholy invalid" who, despite his disabilities, somehow or other managed to compose. That he was born with a predisposition to pulmonary phthisis, which he inherited from his father, is undoubtedly true; but it was not until his twenty-ninth year—when he was subjected to damp and exposure— that it developed. How much the exigencies of Madame George Sand, with whom he was living in Majorca at the time, contributed to the aggravation of his malady, is a matter for conjecture. We only know that despite her assumption of innocence, she seems to have been unduly preoccupied with matters of sex, and it is difficult in the circumstances to imagine that Chopin was not involved in that preoccupation. Yet even so, in 1839, the doctor "declared that his patient showed no longer any symptoms of pulmonary affection, but was suffering merely from a slight chronic laryngeal affection, which, although he did not expect to be able to cure it, need not cause any serious alarm."[6] Subsequent to this we hear very little that is unfavorable about Chopin's health until 1847, after which, with fluctuations, it gradually declined until his death.

We have been at some pains to examine the history of Chopin's physical state in order to dispel several misconceptions, which have arisen, through an inability to dissociate his work and character from his health. One writer, for instance, says:

Of a delicate constitution, which eminently affected the character of his mind, he was attacked in 1837 by a pulmonary and asthmatic disease, from which he never recovered, that indisposed, if not inca-pacitated him for appearance in public, and thus concentrated his thoughts upon composition, *while it tinged them with a peculiar, not to say, morbid expression, which gives marked individuality to every-thing he wrote.** [my italics]

But the author of this monograph is confounding effect and cause. First, disease can never be the cause of a man's creative individuality, otherwise one would only need to infect the most mediocre *dilettante* with disease germs in order to transform him into a genius; second, Chopin was a highly individual composer long before 1837; third, as we shall attempt to show, his compositions, with few exceptions, were not morbid. Yet this writer is only one out of many who thus describes them, for we find the same charge in Huneker's very interesting and significant study. He writes,

Chopin's moods are often morbid, his music often pathological; Beethoven, too, is morbid but in his kingdom so vast, so varied, the mood is lost or lightly felt, while in Chopin's province it looms a maleficent upas-tree, with flowers of evil and its leaves glistening with sensuousness. . . . Chopin has surprised the musical malady of the century. He is its chief spokesman.[7]

Huneker then goes on to bracket him with Nietzsche, and tells us they "both suffered mortally from hyperaesthesia, the penalty of all sick genius." It is true that when a critic speaks of "surprising the musical malady of the century," we cannot refute his statement, because we do not know what it means, but with the imputation of morbidity it is otherwise. Let us seek to discover upon what it was based.

Chopin was the musical poet par excellence of refinement not a super-ficial, but an inner refinement of soul; this refinement, carried, perhaps, in his personal character to excess, was the character and keynote of his music, and it is this that in certain phases has been mistaken for morbidity.

---

*Signed G. A. M.

We have spoken of tone poets in a broad sense, but Chopin was the first tone poet in the truest and most specific sense; and for this reason there is in his music at times, and in varying degrees, that aroma of sadness, which is the quintessence of all genuine lyric poetry. To understand this fact is to understand the personality of Chopin and the influence he had on the world. This refined expression of sadness and sad expression of refinement, although it could alone emanate from a very sensitive organism, was due to an inherent poetic nature, and *not* to a disease of the lungs. And as for that nature itself, it was a blending of French and Polish culture, coloured with a strong vein of patriotism, which did not fail to manifest itself in his music. But again in this there was nothing morbid: as many other composers have derived inspiration from the folk music of their own nation and translated it into their works, so did Chopin, and inevitably with it some of its sadness—for the Polish folk song happens to be sad.

And yet even so, the poetic and languid melancholy of Chopin's muse had assumed undue proportions in the minds of his critics. There is a movement, a vigour, a gaiety in the bulk of his finer compositions, which is the very reverse of sad, though, owing to this inner refinement, which we have stressed, neither his vigour nor his gaiety ever verges on the "muscular" or the boisterous. However animated, however gay, however passionate even, there is a grace of manner, a poetic restraint not to be found in the works of any antecedent composer, except perhaps his contemporary, Mendelssohn, who most nearly approached him in this respect.

Chopin was not only a poet but a musical aristocrat in the most cultured sense of the word; and every one of his emotions he expressed *as* an aristocrat, in the best chosen language. His music was simply the replica idealized of himself; he hated everything blatant, everything that savoured of the unaesthetic. For the dissipations of the "average sensual man he had an abiding contempt."[8] Even his aversion to smoking was because it offended his sense of refinement, and it was this same sense that made public performance and applause odious to him.[9]

His musical tastes were no less revolutionary. Save for one or two sonatas, he did not find Beethoven's work altogether sympathetic: the musical personality of a man who, in front of ladies, could pick his teeth with the candle-snuffers,[10] could hardly be expected to appeal to his delicate nature. Although he admired Beethoven's genius, many of his compositions seemed to him "too rudely sculptured . . . too athletic . . . too tempestuous, their passion too overpowering . . . for his taste."[11]

Nor did Schubert fare much better in his estimation; "in spite of the charm which he acknowledged in some of his melodies," he found him, on the whole, too crude to be pleasant; for all "savage wildness," all unmasked expression of sorrow, was repulsive to him. Indeed, in reviewing Chopin's sympathies, hardly a musician could be instanced with whom they were more exclusive. There were for him but two musical gods—one was Mozart, the other Bach—and he loved the former because in Liszt's words "Mozart condescended more rarely than any other composer to cross the steps which separate refinement from vulgarity." How illuminating this sentence is in connection with Chopin's character!

Except for attempting to dispel those few misconceptions already mentioned, we have purposely avoided saying anything hitherto unsaid about this illustrious Polish musician; we have set down nothing relative to his music, which has not been written and felt by every writer of discernment. And this is as important in estimating his influence on the world as it has been in connection with the other composers dealt with in this book.

We do not, like Lombroso appears to have done, wish to invent "facts" in order to bolster up our contentions. That Chopin was a lunatic there is no existing document to prove, but that he was "the poet of the piano," a "musical aristocrat," inevitably struck every unprejudiced person who heard his music. What failed to strike them, however— for none of them possessed the requisite occult knowledge—was that Chopin was an unconscious medium. Not a medium for disembodied entities, nor yet for every variety of human emotion and passion, but for the aspirations, longings, and thwarted spiritual desires of the intelligentsia of his day. These he reflected and then expressed in terms of music. It is this fact that in part explains the many conflicting notions about his temperament. Although fundamentally he was neither morose nor morbid, being a medium he was inevitably a "man of moods."

12

Chopin, the Pre-Raphaelites, and the Emancipation of Women

Chopin's music was of the type that had an almost instantaneous effect; but by this we do not mean that the plenitude of its influence was reached immediately; at the outset it merely affected the more sensitive organisms, until later on it became generally diffused. In the domain of painting it indirectly inspired the Pre-Raphaelite Brotherhood and Burne-Jones; in the domain of literature, the stylistic refinements of Flaubert, Rossetti, Paul Verlaine, Maeterlinck, and others.

Chopin visited England for the first time in 1837, and by 1843 his works were sufficiently known to prompt the English critic, J. W. Davison, to publish a book on the subject. Some few years later the Pre-Raphaelite Brotherhood was formed.

Into the technical doctrines of that Brotherhood we need not enter; it is the spirit of their work with which we are concerned, a spirit which is at once the quintessence of refinement, of aestheticism, of poetical minutiae. There is in many of the pictures, especially in those of Rossetti—as also of Burne-Jones—that same refined languor, that same delicacy of outline to be found so frequently in Chopin's melodies. Had the latter introduced, instead of Polish dance-music, the archaic flavor of plain song into his work, the analogy would be complete. As it was, only the Chopinesque spirit came to be imbibed by the above-mentioned painters, the manner they adopted from the early Italian school. So transparent, in fact, must this be to all who have allowed themselves to sense the atmosphere of a Pre-Raphaelite picture, that it seems unnecessary to elaborate further. Suffice it to add that some of the Pre-Raphaelites and their offshoots carried refinement to such lengths that it gave rise to that portrayal of "passionless, pallid maidens" and bloodless knights, which provoked the "literary wrath" of the Jewish philosopher Nordau, and impelled him to maintain that practically all the art and literature of his day was the result of physical and psychical degeneration.

If we turn from Pre-Raphaelite painting to Pre-Raphaelite literature, in which the names of Rossetti, William Morris, and Maeterlinck predominate, in each of these men, despite their predilection for medievalism, the same spirit of refinement prevails. Whatever the emotion depicted, there is a complete absence of brutality. Some of the medieval ballads proper, for instance, are intensely brutal—not so the balladistic poetry of Morris or Rossetti, or the romantic dramas of Maeterlinck. The romance of "Aglavaine and Selysette," by the latter, in which a young woman commits suicide so that her betrothed may marry another woman, is intrinsically Chopinesque in its delicacy of treatment. None of the directness of Shakespeare or Beethoven is to be found in this tragedy, and the same applies to every drama Maeterlinck wrote. Over all there is a veil of chaste simplicity, of simple restraint; it is one of the phases of the Chopin spirit carried to its extreme limit.

Nor do we fail to perceive its influence in the poetry of Ernest Dowson and Paul Verlaine; there is that same exquisite refinement in all their works. Although passion is not missing from some of Dowson's lyrics, it is always enshrouded in an atmosphere of roses and violets, of softness and shadows; "blood and thunder" was as foreign to Dowson as it was to Chopin himself. And then if we consider Flaubert—that novelist who was so tortured by the exigencies of refinement of style that hours would pass while he weighed the appropriateness of one word—stylistic refinement with him had assumed the proportions of a malady.

The influence of Chopin upon manners was as pronounced if not as apparent as his influence upon literature and art. If we revert for a moment to Handel, we will remember that *he* inspired conventionality and propriety. The outward manifestation of his influence is expressible in such phrases as: "Other people don't do it, neither must we," or, more concisely put: "It isn't *done*. . . ." Thus, as the outcome of Handel's influence anything in the nature of coarseness, for example, was considered *wrong;* as the outcome of Chopin's influence it was considered "*not nice*": the anti-conventional, therefore reprehensible, had become the unaesthetic. But not only had Chopin's music an aestheticizing effect, it had also and inevitably a selective one: the *they* became the *we.* No longer was it a question of what other people do, or the reverse, it was a question of what *we* do, or the reverse—we who are the *elite* and who are separate from the mass. Thus Chopin was, at any rate, responsible for a step in the right direction; he had altered and refined the motive. That people should refrain from doing a thing because it was unbeautiful was better than that they should merely refrain because it was unconventional.

There was nevertheless an unpleasant side to the picture, for this idea of "*we,* the *élite,*" gave rise to a certain snobbishness, and consequently to a pronounced degree of intolerance—it was Chopin's own exclusiveness manifesting itself. In its most aggravated form it produced cliquism; in its higher form it inspired the inauguration of societies connected with intellectual or artistic pursuits. Thus, we find that in 1854 an Act was passed "to afford facilities for the establishment of institutions for the promotion of literature and science by grants of land, etc., and for their regulation." From that time onward, the number of societies devoted to art, music, or *belles lettres* and formed in London alone, is particularly striking. Beginning with the Society for the Encouragement of Fine Arts (1858), we may enumerate among others the Early English Texts Society, Chaucer Society, Holbein Society, New Shakespeare Society, Musical Association, Purcell Society, Hellenic Society, Carlyle Society, Wordsworth Society, Browning Society, London Dante Society, Ruskin

Society, Shelley Society, Goethe Society, Elizabethan Society, and so on. It will be seen that a special feature of these societies was that most of them were formed around the name of one particular man—a poet or musician; this except where religion was concerned, was something new. Hitherto, people had been content to read their especially cherished poets at home in solitary pleasure, but after Chopin had diffused his influence, they formed themselves into societies in order, on the one hand, to gain a better understanding of their poetic idols, and on the other, so that they might feel that *they* knew and comprehended them better than "the man in the street"—it was again a question of the *we*—*we* who are more cultivated than our fellows!

Chopin's influence upon women was especially appreciable in Germany and England. Neither the German nor the English women of the period were, as a general rule, mentally cultured; they were good housewives, they embroidered, they knitted, they crocheted, they were proficient in what was called "deportment," and to a limited extent they played the piano and sang innocuous drawing-room ditties. But even so, these accomplishments were largely inspired by an *arrière pensée*— the desirability of marriage. They were not the *insignia* of an aspiration towards true mind or soul culture; they were merely the essential ingredients which went to the fashioning of an "eligible young woman." Indeed, in the Victorian era a mentally cultured woman was regarded as a conjugal inconvenience—husbands, being none too intellectual themselves, were apprehensive of being allocated to a position of inferiority. Let women be beautiful and "accomplished," but not too intelligent: this was the attitude which that obtained.

The influence of Chopin was destined to alter it in a manner of which no other musician was capable. The conventionalising effects of Handel had but augmented it, they only inspired more reverence and awe on the part of women towards their husbands and consequently towards their wishes and opinions. As most people are aware, there was, in the Victorian era, seldom any true friendship between husbands and wives. The men feared God, the women feared God *and* their husbands; it therefore became necessary that a subtler influence should be employed to break down this debilitating dependency—that influence, as already said, was Chopin. He affected women—though unbeknown to themselves—through his refinement, his delicacy, his aestheticism. Through that feminine absence of all that was harsh, rough, or grating, his music insinuated itself into their subconscious minds and left its cultural imprint—it was like one tenderly feminine soul speaking to another and gently firing it with nobler aspirations. Alone the music of a man who "never made use of an inelegant word, even in moments of the most entire familiarity . . . whose gaiety was always restrained within the limits of perfect good taste"[1]—only the music of such a man could be calculated not to wound the susceptibilities of those delicate Victorian organisms. Beethoven, direct and ruthless, with his psychoanalytical powers, had liberated a multitude of repressed passions from the subconscious, but apart from sympathy he had, so to speak, left nothing in their place. His had been an emptying process; to Chopin it was allotted to fill the void. As Beethoven had awakened that sympathy by portraying the tragedies and sordidness of life, so did Chopin awaken the desire for culture by portraying the poetry of refinement and the inherent charm of poetry itself. The result was that women who had been perfectly content to stay at home and make antimacassars for the household chairs or carpet slippers for prospective or present husbands, began to join societies for the better understanding of poetry or the fine arts. It was the beginning of the emancipation of womanhood.

There are some who are disposed to belittle Chopin because he did not paint, as it were, on large canvases and with a stronger brush. Such people, however, are merely voicing a pseudo-rational excuse for their temperamental inability to appreciate the exquisite. Chopin was a musical inventor of the first degree, who enriched the musical vocabulary of his time to such a marked extent that few subsequent composers have failed to profit thereby.*

From the occult point of view there were definite reasons why he did not and could not use the large canvas nor reach heights of inspiration

---

*Strains of Chopinesque device are even noticeable in so comparatively recent a composer as Richard Strauss.

sufficiently imposing to satisfy his modern critics. These reasons were in part connected with his personal limitations and in part with the collective limitations of his day. Most forms of inspiration come from the higher planes or from contact with the Devas,* but this in itself inevitably produces a reaction upon the physical body. Had Chopin been subjected to sustained inspiration of this nature, his frail physique would have been incapable of enduring the strain, and not only would his death have eventuated sooner than it actually did, but his music would have been incomprehensible to an as yet unprepared world.

Before we complete this chapter, a word should be added relative to another composer whose influence on culture was very marked, namely Georges Bizet. As Chopin was the poet of refinement for the piano, Bizet was the poet of refinement for the orchestra. Born just eleven years before the death of the Polish musician, he carried on the work which the latter had begun, until his own death in 1875. It is safe to say that prior to Bizet no orchestrator had manifested such a consistent sense for instrumental euphony. Berlioz in comparison was a bombastic thunderer, and Beethoven, with his unfortunate use of the trumpets, left much to be desired. Even Mendelssohn did not come up to the standard of Bizet: he painted with a heavier brush. But then, it would seem that in order to understand the true essence of euphonious sonority, one must need be born a Frenchman. Bizet, in spite of his predilection for "local colour," was French through and through—he possessed all the French charm, all the French polish—as the hackneyed phrase goes, like French women, he was *toujours chic.* And yet he could be both tragic and dramatic, as witness at the end of *Carmen* the last agonized cry of Don José. Nevertheless, with all his sense of tragedy, Bizet never became heavy or vulgarly melodramatic. Moreover, he never lost his sense of the beautiful; with him passion and power were seldom if ever portrayed by harshness, they were portrayed by yet another phase of beauty.

---

*For the benefit of non-theosophical readers the Devas are a graded hierarchy of incorporeal Beings ranging from the smallest nature-spirit to the loftiest archangel (see chapter 16).

13

Robert Schumann and the Child-Nature

It is a noticeable fact that a vast change has taken place relative to the education of children. The first signs of this change were already perceptible after 1836, when Froebel opened his Kindergarten school at Blankenberghe. But that the Kindergarten became a popular institution was in part due to the influence of Robert Schumann's music, which began to find favour about that time, while much later on the Montessori system was, we learn, actually inspired by that influence. It crystallised at last the realisation (1) that children are all different from one another, and hence must be treated individually and not en masse; (2) that children cannot in reality be educated by anyone else, "the impulse to learn must come from within their own minds"; (3) that children are so constituted that *given proper conditions they prefer educating themselves to any other occupation.*"[1]

For in these three sentences are clothed the underlying ideas of that system, which is more and more obtaining a hold with those who have the interests of children at heart.

But of course where it was possible for such a practical measure to be introduced, let alone accepted, a marked alteration in the prevailing attitude towards children was highly essential. During the Victorian epoch not only was the treatment of the young based on a remarkable

ignorance of human nature, but on an equally remarkable, if unconscious, selfishness. Children were to be "seen and not heard," which
meant that they were to afford an ocular pleasure to adults, but were
not to inconvenience them by asking questions, still less by romping
and making a noise. That Nature, in order to develop their lungs and
muscles, requires that children *should* romp and shout, did not sufficiently occur to our Victorian forefathers; nor that they *must* ask questions in order to acquire knowledge. For young people to behave thus
was not consistent with that idea of awe and reverence, which ought
to be observed before elders and betters! But of course children did
romp and shout and ask questions nevertheless, because Nature is more
powerful than precept, and the result very often was chastisement, justified by the wisdom of Solomon, no allowance being made for Oriental
hyperbole. In a word, children were treated after the manner of criminals; they were *punished,* not *reformed.* It was for the influence of
Robert Schumann to bring about that deeper love and understanding
of the child, which among the intelligentsia is such a pronounced characteristic of the present age.

Many years ago one frequently heard the expression "a literary
painter"; it appeared to denote a man who was as much preoccupied
with the subject he painted as with the painting itself. This expression,
if we mistake not, has been applied to Burne-Jones, Rossetti, Böcklin,
and others, because they combined poetry of subject with beauty of
representation. The analogy of this in the realm of the tonal art is to be
found in the composer of what is termed "programme music" in contradistinction to the composer of *absolute* music—the one aims at expressing an emotion, a scene or an idea, the other is content to "express
nothing but music itself"—if such a thing were possible.

Now, although Schumann never actually wrote symphonic poems,
his inspiration was more influenced by literature than that of any composer we have hitherto examined. One may even go so far as to say it
was almost entirely nourished on the writings of Jean Paul. So great
was his admiration for this author "that he would become violently
angry if anyone ventured to doubt or criticize Jean Paul's greatness as

an imaginative writer."[2] Nor was Schumann's estimation of him unjustified, for interspersed among his interminable novels are to be found, clothed in the form of dreams, the most remarkable and grandiose prose-poems that have ever evolved; they are cosmic in their grandeur, and Carlyle, as well as Schumann, was enmeshed in their enthralment. But then Schumann was a dreamer himself; he was also a poet in embryo; for at one time "his inclinations seem almost to have hung in the balance between music and literature."[3] As it was, the two became closely intermingled; he not only adopted the avocation of musical *litterateur,* but was the first *literary* composer of whom there is any record.* With him the title of a piece was, if not an essential adjunct, at any rate an aid to its comprehension. And yet—significant fact— the piece was conceived first and the fitting title afterwards; which goes to show that Schumann, instead of circumscribing his musical inspiration by a literary idea, allowed the former to have full sway: it was, as it were, the voice of music which spoke first, it was that same voice that ultimately conveyed to him its own meaning.

And it is just that meaning, or rather multitude of meanings conveyed through Schumann's vast number of pieces, from which one may gain some idea of the content of his message. That it is not as immediately apparent as that of Handel, Bach, or Chopin must be admitted; but if we approach Schumann's music with a sufficiently unprejudiced mind, *his* message is discernible nonetheless.

In the first place an atmosphere of simplicity and innocence pervades practically the whole of his works, whether he portrays the scenes of childhood or the sentiments of adults. In the second place he entertained a noticeable predilection for simple forms: the song form so-called, the theme and variations, and the song proper. Even his larger dimensional works, quartets and symphonies, are mostly composed of song-form sections. As for the *Carnival* and the *Papillons,* they are a series of small pieces placed together under one comprehensive title. It was not that Schumann did not aspire towards the more

---

*We here distinguished between *literary* and *operatic.*

architectural type of forms in which Beethoven and Mendelssohn had excelled, it was that this inherent *simplicity* always asserted itself, no matter what he wrote. Indeed, since Domenico Scarlatti and the Clavecinists, never had a serious composer written such a prodigious number of small pieces. If we glance through the thirty-four volumes of Schumann's works we find *Papillons* (twelve pieces), *Davidsbündler* (eighteen pieces), *Kinderszenen* (thirteen pieces), *Bunte Blätter* (fourteen pieces), *Novelletten* (eight pieces), and so on; only now and then do we stray upon an overture, a sonata, or a symphony. And then, if we study the titles, there is the same poetic simplicity, as if Schumann were deliberately naming his creations to suit the child-mind. Thus "Scenes of Childhood," "Motley Leaves," "Butterflies," "Fairy-tale Pictures," "Fairy Stories," "Children's Ball," "Album for the Young," and "Christmas Album." And again, such significant superscriptions for single pieces as "Why?" "Happiness is Enough," "Soaring," "The Merry Peasant," and so forth. Moreover, Schumann takes care to explain to his friends the meaning of some of his titles; he distinguishes the *Kinderszenen* for instance, from the *Weihnachtsalbum* "on the grounds that the former are the recollections, which a grown man retains of his childhood, while the latter consists of imaginings and expectations of young people."[4]

Schumann has been termed the Musical Apostle of the Romantic Movement, and the phrase is apt enough, but with him true romance was associated with childhood, not with maturity. Himself a large overgrown child, a dreamer, he portrayed those romantic sentiments that alone exist in the dreamland of children. Who but a big child, fond of fanciful pranks, could have conceived of and enjoyed such a strange creation as the *Davidsbündler*? Here was a purely fictitious brotherhood, half humorous, half poetical, which existed solely in the imagination of Schumann himself.[5] It was but an elaboration of the childish fondness for games of pretence. And this being so, we cannot fail to see whence Schumann's idolization of Jean Paul arose, for the latter "was unsurpassed in depicting the tender emotions with his dazzling and even extravagant play of digressive fancy, his excess of feeling over dramatic power, his incessant alternations between laughter and tears."[6]

Yet, withal, Schumann lacked the *power* of Jean Paul's greatest moments. When Schumann tried to be strong, he usually succeeded alone in portraying the strength of a little boy pretending to be a big one. There is always something intrinsically naive about these attempts, for if he does manage to invent a bold, clear-cut theme, as the first theme of the B-flat symphony, for example, it invariably, after a few bars, breaks off into something either playful or pleading. Another childlike element in Schumann is his predilection for telling stories, or, at any rate, "for bringing his hearers into a condition of mind from which they could go on romancing for themselves."[7] He has also a great fondness for musical jokes, whimsicalities, and puzzles: not only did he write six fugues on the name "Bach" but a whole set of variations on a theme formed from the letters of a young lady's name. Further instances of this type of playfulness may be found in the *Carnival,* in the "Album for the Young," and in other works.

In passing at length from causes to effects, we must once again emphasise the fact that music speaks its message direct to the heart. Schumann was—as it were—the messenger from the heart of the child to the heart of the parent. Nay, he was more: he was the true poet of the child-soul, of the child-nature, of the child-life. With his tenderness, his whimsicality amid his humour; with his questionings, his fancifulness, his pleadings, and his dreaminess, he implanted in the mother-heart the true likeness of the child—and she understood. Children were different from what she had previously thought. Her own childhood, though remembered, had taught her very little, in spite of its multitude of joys and sorrows. She had been corrected and punished, and had arrived at what she now was; what had been good enough for her when she was a child would be good enough for other children. But now a subtle influence told her otherwise. Children were not all alike, they were as varied as adults; there was only one similarity between them: that they were all children. It was our treatment of them that made them appear all alike; we allowed them no self-expression, we trampled upon their individualities, we silenced their questionings, we never tried to understand them, to foster their latent faculties, to discover their latent talents. When they were naughty we punished and put them to bed, but we never sought to find out the true cause of their naughtiness and wisely to remedy it; on the contrary, we resorted to the expedient of frightening them. Was there no better way?

So far we have considered the effect of Schumann's music on adults, but it had, or rather *has,* a marked effect on children themselves; it helps the child more speedily to reach maturity of mind. There are children born nowadays who astonish their elders by their spasmodic outbursts of wisdom. This precocity is in a large measure due to Schumann's influence; for, owing to the improvement in the conditions of child-life, the latent faculties of the child-soul are brought more readily into manifestation. His music affects the *subconsciousness* of children in a manner in which none hitherto has been capable of affecting it. It is the only music so far conceived, which is attuned to the child-mind, and for this reason it is—equally—the only music capable of *educating* the child. The musical soul of Schumann, so to say, understood the soul of the child, and spoke to it as no other composer *could* speak . . . and he spoke to it with tenderness and love.

Like Chopin, Robert Schumann has exercised a marked effect on the pictorial art; he was, for one thing, largely responsible for that type, which in its first form was known as the *Jugendstil,* the very word *Jugend* meaning youth. It was in evidence in the final decade of the last century, but since then it has undergone development at the hands of a variety of artists. But even more has Schumann been responsible for moulding the post-impressionist painters, and many of those who have followed. If we examine the spirit of post-impressionism, we must inevitably notice that its outstanding feature is naiveté, and the drawings and paintings inspired by its influence look as if they had been executed by *children*—trees, houses, figures, all suggest the hand and mind of a child. This is already noticeable in the works of Gauguin and Van Gogh; it is even more noticeable in the works of Picasso. This primitiveness, this simplicity of conception, has spread far and wide into all countries; in Switzerland we notice it in the paintings of Hodler, we notice it in

German, French, English, Russian, and Italian painters, and we do not hesitate to repeat that it was indirectly inspired by Schumann, as the pre-Raphaelites were indirectly inspired by Chopin. That it took longer to materialise, we admit; but then Schumann's music has never been quite so extensively played as that of Chopin.

Summing up, one may say that although the more direct effects of the great romanticist's music have been beneficial, not so some of its more indirect effects. Admittedly certain childlike elements in art have their beauty and attractiveness but when carried to extremes are apt to become absurd and suggestive of bad workmanship. Finding that the childlike tendencies in painting could be exploited, quite a number of present-day painters and draftsmen have affected a childish style, which, though meant to be taken seriously, is merely an unpleasant type of caricature. Thus, a fashion for deliberate bad drawing has been created together with other characteristics suggestive of the nursery. Such art, although it may occasion a transient sensation, is not destined to live; it would seem to be one of those symptoms denoting a deficiency of true inspiration.

14
The Effects of Wagner's Music

In the year 1855 the Directors of the old Philharmonic Society in London were at some pains to find a new conductor; Spohr, Sterndale Bennett, and Berlioz were not available, while less eminent men were hardly suited to the dignity of such a post. After some deliberation, however, a composer-conductor was transported from Zurich, and on March 12 he reaped "an undoubted triumph" from a highly astonished audience, as well as from the orchestra itself. The Press was also astonished, but its astonishment was of another nature; "it turned upon this fine-profiled, alert little gentleman" with unanimity, which it very seldom displays, and excited itself almost to hysteria over the "mass of incoherent rubbish, which he had the temerity to offer as a contribution to art."[1] One writer informed the public that he was "a desperate charlatan endowed with worldly skill and vigorous purpose enough to persuade a gaping crowd that the nauseous compound he manufactures has some precious inner virtue, which they must live and ponder yet ere they perceive . . ." Further, that "scarcely the most ordinary ballad-writer but would shame him in the creation of melody, and no English harmonist of more than one year's growth could be found sufficient without ears and understanding to pen such vile things." Another writer appears to have warned his readers that if they listened to the impious theories, the "wily eloquence" of this new conductor-composer, they would "find themselves in the coils of rattlesnakes," for his compositions were "reckless, wild, extravagant, and demagogic cacophony, the symbol of profligate libertinage."[2]

Meanwhile Richard Wagner, the individual who provoked these instructive obloquies, continued to conduct the Philharmonic; he was in his forty-second year. Not so very long afterward, members of the public paid £5 for a ticket to hear *Tannhäuser*.

But although it is true, as Hadow points out, that Wagner had omitted to call on the critics, there are deeper reasons for this "singular lack of urbanity" on the part of these musical journalists. Those Dark Powers, which work *against* the spiritual evolution of the race, were using every means at their disposal to thwart Wagner and his message— the critics were an easy prey for their endeavours—and they employed them. And we need not search far for the reason: criticism, as practised by journalists, is usually destructive; and like attracts like.

Wagner's life had been one of continuous struggle; exiled from Germany on account of revolutionary opinions, he had in Paris, where he had fled, faced a condition verging on starvation. Nevertheless, he had already written seven operas and sketched parts of the eighth and ninth: namely the *Walküre* and *Siegfried*. In these latter, and in the *Rheingold,* which he completed in May 1854, the true creative spirit in Wagner was made manifest.

Those who have read Bernard Shaw's ingenious interpretation of the *Rheingold* will, as far as its plot is concerned, have gained some idea of its socialistic meaning, if not of its more transcendental one, though the two are closely interwoven. They will also have realised on fairly sound evidence that Wagner himself was less clear as to his own meaning than was his interpreter. For there is a letter written to his friend Roeckel in which he says that an artist "feels in the presence of his work, if it be true art, that he is confronted by a riddle about which he, too, might have illusions . . ." Again, in another letter: "I believe a true instinct has kept me from too great a definiteness, for it has been borne in on me that an absolute disclosure of the intentions disturbs true insight." And finally: "You must feel that something is being enacted that is not to be expressed in mere words." And these confessions are significant from the occult standpoint, for they tend to show that Wagner was used by forces extraneous to himself, as we shall see later.

Now, the keynote to Wagner's music-drama is unity in diversity. In the old-fashioned opera each number—involving a different melody—was separate and apart; but with Wagner on the contrary, although there are a vast array of themes, melodies and *motifs,* they are woven together in such wise as to present one continuous whole. Thus, we see at the outset that a profound spiritual principle underlay his entire constructional scheme: the many were blended together in the one. As the waves of the ocean are each different—having a different form—yet are nevertheless one with it and inseparable from it, so each melody, though individual, was one with the great artwork of which it formed a part. Socialistically speaking, Wagner's music was the prototype of the principle of co-operation in contradistinction to competition; spiritually speaking, it symbolised the mystic truth that each individual soul is unified with the All-soul, the All-pervading Consciousness.

Such then was Wagner's constructional scheme; but in order to form this great scheme he had to break down many pre-existent musical conventions. In vain did the pedagogues of music look for adherence to their cherished rules of harmony, and for their neatly rounded-off and applause-inviting arias. In vain did they look for correct modulations and resolutions, and all the other technical appurtenances of the nineteenth century? In place of them they found unresolved discords, *false relations,* and transitions into keys which had no perceptible connection with the key just abandoned—all was seeming lawlessness, deliberate disregard of rule and precedent—scandalous *Freedom*! Yet, with this apparent lawlessness, what was Wagner actually accomplishing? In order to attain unity, he was breaking down the *barriers* to unity, and so setting music free.

But although he introduced such marked structural innovations in operatic form, it is not solely to these we must look for the far-reaching effects he was destined to produce. Beethoven had portrayed human love, Bach and Handel had portrayed religious devotion or love *for* God, but Wagner was the first to portray that Love, which *is* God, the Divine Love or what in certain schools of occultism is termed the Buddhic. There are three operatic sections in which Wagner's inspiration reached and lingered at this sublime altitude—in the *Preislied,* in the *Liebestod* at the end of *Tristan,* and in the *Karfreitagszauber* in *Parsifal.* The first was sung by Walther in the *Meistersinger* and was inspired by his love for Eva; the other two were inspired by Wagner's own love for Mathilde Wesendonck.* Yet although these *scenas* may thus have been inspired by love of a personal nature, the outcome was the expression of a sublimation of that love: a transformation of it into the Divine.

These rare flights of Wagner's to the Buddhic plane have not been without momentous results on those people capable of responding to their lofty vibrations. For these, too, have momentarily been transported to that exalted plane, and raised to that state of Unity, of selfless unconditional Love. Into their hearts in consequence has been instilled the ideal of Brotherhood and the desirability of bringing it into manifestation.

We have singled out three passages in Wagner's operas as the highest ones, yet only the Initiate is in a position to *know* the spiritual value or altitude of a given piece of music; noninitiates can only *feel* it and judge by the *effects* on themselves. A hint, nonetheless, may be put forward. Those who are able clairaudiently to hear the music of the higher spheres, hear not only one melody, but countless melodies simultaneously and all are blending together in subtle but perfect harmony. The music of earth, which most closely resembles that of these higher planes, possesses the greatest spiritual value. Thus, when the ingenuity of a composer is such that he can interblend several beautiful melodies so that they can be played simultaneously to produce one harmonious whole, then the spirituality of his music is assured. But there are yet other ways, one being to clothe his melodic outline in chords, i.e., instead of his melodies being composed of single notes or octaves,

---

*The music of the *Karfreitagszauber* was written during the Wesendonck episode and later on embodied in *Parsifal.*

like those of Tchaikovsky, they may be composed of chords so that each single note of the chords, when played in succession, forms a melody of itself. In the *Liebestod,* Wagner adopted to a certain extent this latter method; in the end of the *Götterdammerung,* for instance, he adopted the former one. With regard to the *Karfreitagszauber* and the *Preislied,* in these the melodies themselves are expressive of that divine Peace, which constitutes the all-pervading essence of super-earthly planes; they are not so much an echo of the music of those planes as an expression of their love-fragranced beatitude.

Some of the effects of these spiritual portions in Wagner's music have already come into manifestation, for all those movements, having unity or brotherhood as their ideal, are the result of his influence. The diffusion of Theosophy, which demands that its adherents should accept the great ideal of Brotherhood but leaves them free in every other respect, may be mentioned as one of these results. Before Wagner's day a religion founded on the tolerant principle that its devotees might "believe anything they liked" would have been regarded as preposterous and totally impracticable.

We have finally to deal with the less desirable effects of the Wagnerian music. To the better understanding of these, however, it is necessary to remember that Wagner was first and foremost an artist and a dramatist who realised, and naturally so, that neither a dramatic nor musical creation is possible without its due proportion of contrast. Thus, the portrayal both in text and music of a great many ugly emotions was inevitable. Yet had Wagner been a less forceful composer, the effects accruing from these would have been negligible. As it was, they served to intensify the corresponding emotions in large numbers of his compatriots, especially that love of power, which played such an important part in the *Nibelungen Ring.* Nevertheless, its results would have been less pronounced had not Wagner's music, as a whole, contained such a strong element of the Germanic. The latter, coupled with the equally strong elements of the romantic and the heroic, aroused in the Germans themselves that feeling of intense nationalism for which they became notorious. They had always been sentimental about the country of their birth, but now they saw it and themselves through a haze of glory. Add to this gratifying vision love of power, and the outcome was *Deutschland über alles,* the apotheosis of Germany.

The disastrous upshot of this requires little comment. Had Wagner's music been less "German," had the Buddhic element in it preponderated, had the bulk of the German people been sufficiently evolved to respond to its lofty vibrations, they would have denounced War as the uncivilised and futile thing it really is. As for the Second World War, it must be admitted that the uncritical hero-worship of the man Hitler was a pronounced factor in bringing it about. And unfortunately there were certain elements in the Wagnerian opera-plots, which were conducive to this folly we call hero worship, seeing that many of the personalities thus worshiped are far from being true heroes. It is stated that Hitler himself was a great lover of Wagner, the reason being that he dramatised himself as a "Siegfried." Had he been a nobler character and not the megalomaniac that he was, he would have responded to the loftier phases of Wagner's music instead of leading his adulators to their destruction, because obsessed by his own importance, nationalism, Germany, and the *Herrenvolk* delusion.*

The adventurous and complex life of Richard Wagner obviously cannot be compressed into a few sentences, nor can the complexities of his character. Therefore, suffice it here to mention one thing that had a marked effect on his music. That he possessed one outstanding desire, namely the formation of a great brotherhood of art, is conclusively proven; and that when through the ridicule of the Press and other opposition he found it unrealisable, the truth nearly shattered his frame, has also been proven. "His whole life, in fact, was single-heartedly devoted to the regeneration of the human race, and in art he saw the means of its accomplishment."[3] Moreover, as this aspiration implies, he loved not

---

*It has been pointed out by the Master who modestly calls Himself "The Tibetan," that the combats, which materialized as the two Great Wars, were inevitable at the end of the Picean Age; but if Humanity had been less contentious and not made such bad karma, they could have been "fought out" on the *Mental Plane,* in which case all the frightful slaughter and destruction would have been avoided.

only the human race, but the brute creation also, his letters being full of charming references to domestic animals, not to mention that "one of his most trenchant essays is directed towards vivisection."[4]

It was because Wagner possessed such a strong desire to help mankind that he earned the right to be used, even if only intermittently, by the Masters, who recognized in him the finest musical medium They were likely to have for the next fifty years or so. We have, however, no evidence to show that he was aware of this overshadowing, nor of the fact that he was also, and very extensively, used by the Devas (see chapter 16),which in itself is enough to account for traits in his character, which have called forth such strong criticism from some of his later biographers. For it often happens that Deva-inspired people lose their sense of proportion and their sense of values, and become imbued with what appears to be an intense egoism and selfishness. This is largely because the Devas themselves, or at any rate those in question, are not only intensely one-pointed, but have little knowledge of the customs, limitations, and ethics of our human existence. Such an attribute as modesty is unknown to them, as also and equally its antithesis, conceit, for neither of these play any part in their own ethereal organisms. To "get their message across" is all that concerns them, and to this end they allow their agents no respite. Thus the character, which Wagner showed to the world, was not exclusively his own; it was in part that of the lesser National Devas who dominated him, hence a distortion, half-human, half-Devic.

And so it is in occultism, finally, that we discover the solution to that psychological puzzle, which has so often given rise to the question, why men of genius are not invariably men of the highest moral integrity.

15
Richard Strauss and Individualism

The music of Richard Strauss, despite its individuality and its technical inventiveness, possesses without a doubt a very close kinship with that of Wagner. It is, in fact, an extension, an intensification of certain phases of the Wagnerian genius. Strauss might best be described as Wagner in a greater degree technically speaking, and in a lesser degree aesthetically and *spiritually* speaking. He has increased, so to say, the Wagnerian harmonic vocabulary—already an enormous one, seeing that Wagner's inventiveness in this direction was unprecedented, he intensified his exuberance, but he never reached those rarefied spiritual ethers to which his illustrious predecessor attained. Whether in *Salome*, for instance, Strauss was aiming at the portrayal of an intrinsically spiritual character with his music descriptive of John the Baptist, is difficult to say; it is possible that he was actuated by a none-too-subtle irony at this particular moment. In any case the Johannic characterization-music savours more of Teutonic religious sentimentality than *spirituality;* there is even something weakly Mendelssohn-like about the passage in question. Moreover, other passages where one feels that Strauss might *wish* to be spiritual, only succeed in being *sweet*. And it is a specifically *German* sweetness, for Strauss is even more national than was Wagner. After periods of daring inventiveness, of wild exuberance, of harsh discordancy, he lapses into the most flagrant examples of patriotic tunefulness. The result of this has been to accentuate that German race-feeling, which much of Wagner's music had already been instrumental in emphasising. Strauss not only caused the Germans to feel even more sentimental about their country than had his predecessor, but, by a grandiose portrayal of battle through the medium of music,* he glorified war and strife, creating thereby a thought-form, which was used by the Dark Forces to help precipitate the war itself. Nor did the "untrammelledness" of his music cease to be operative after World War I had come to its unsatisfactory end; for it undoubtedly played its part in producing the revolution that followed, even though the latter was actually brought to a head by the German defeat. Indeed, since his music had become disseminated, revolutions and social upheavals have increased, and all the various *isms* aiming at greater freedom, at greater self-expression, have become more widely diffused. Strauss, with the blending of his daring and anti-conventional harmonies and melodic exuberance, emotionalised humanity in such ways that they aspired to break the bonds and become *free*. The very obviousness of some of Strauss's melodies augmented this emotionalizing effect: his discords alone merely broke down conventional thinking; it was for his easily comprehensible melodies to fire the emotions that eventually inspire *actions*.

That these actions, of course, took various forms, was to be expected; the poet wrote poems with revolutionary or individualistic content; the orator was impelled to use his oratory in the cause of freedom; the writer turned his attention to that same cause; the painter ignored the conventions of all previous painters; and even the sculptor exclaimed: "I will not be bound by nature's dictates!" Thus, to whatever field of activity we look, this craving for *Freedom* becomes increasingly noticeable. What, again, has inspired the outcry respecting the severity of the marriage laws? Why have people at last demanded easier divorce? It is this same aspiration—woman demands the same rights as man— and she is justified in her demands.

---

*Notably in *Ein Heldenleben*.

Nevertheless, this mention of Strauss and Wagner in connection with the loosening of the divorce laws may seem to give substance to an idea entertained by not a few people, namely, that the intensely emotional music of these two composers tends to emphasise the erotic passions, and, therefore, what we have termed freedom should more correctly be termed *libertinage*. And although we repudiate this latter imputation, it must be admitted that there do exist people who become sexually stimulated when hearing the music of Wagner and more especially that of Strauss. For this, however, the nature of those individuals in question is more responsible than the music itself. Music of such force naturally stirs the entire being and touches the lower elements as well as the higher. People with little or nothing of emotional control may therefore be thrown into a state of chaotic excitement by Strauss's music, which, in contradistinction to Wagner's, reaches only the plane of *emotional* and not of *spiritual* love. But on those of controlled temperament and lofty aspirations, no such effects will be perceptible; spiritual love is, as it were, the higher octave of the emotional, and, in natures, capable of feeling such love, the striking of that lower note will immediately be echoed by response from the higher. It should be added, however, that the aforementioned *passional* effects are of a quite transient order.

In England, the first Strauss festival took place in 1903, and since then—except during the First World War—his works have been played more and more frequently. It is also since then that all those freedom-aspiring movements, including militant suffrage, came into prominence. Nevertheless, it is evident from many indications that his music is beginning to be "dated, " and fails to stir the emotions of its listeners as it did formerly. Moreover, Strauss himself changed his musical policy. Since *Electra* he toned down the forcefulness of his Muse and turned more to melodiousness and the immediately appealing. In the *Rosenkavalier,* which followed *Electra,* he derived much of his inspiration from Mozart, thus reverting to the past. With the change in his actual music has come a change in its influence. In his later works, at any rate, he is no longer the Apostle of Freedom, for in some respects he has returned to more conventional forms.

As to the effect that his music will exercise on coming generations; that largely depends on whether the work of the earlier or the later period survives. Meanwhile it is significant that a certain section of the German people have shown a marked desire to return to the old regime. Although in theory a republican government may seem expedient, yet inwardly they incline towards a monarchy as being more romantic and suggestive of rule by a firm hand. Those elements of freedom in Strauss's music, which at one time urged them to rebel against an autocratic government, are losing their effect. After Strauss, German music tended toward the ultra-discordant, so it is perhaps not surprising that the Germans are torn by conflicting political emotions.

Richard Strauss is the last great German musician with whom we propose extensively to deal. It will be noticed that Weber, Schubert, Brahms, and Reger, individual though they were, have been omitted; and the reasons for this are that (1) Weber exercised a greater influence on music itself and on other composers—notably on Chopin and Wagner—than on character and morals; (2) that the effects of Schubert's music, though responsible for instilling sweetness, gentleness, and softness into life, were not sufficiently pronounced to warrant a lengthy survey; (3) that Brahms's music was largely a variant on that of Beethoven and Mendelssohn, i.e. it expressed the higher human emotions and especially inspired sympathy; and finally that Max Reger's influence was similar to that of Bach, with this difference: that by means of his unconventional harmonies he aroused a correspondingly unconventional type of thinking. Of one more composer, Arnold Schönberg, we shall have occasion to speak briefly in our study of the Deva-evolution exponents—a subject that will occupy the third part of this book.

Some readers of the earlier editions of this book have asked me why no mention was made of certain fine and well-recognized composers: Berlioz for one. But the reason is that even some quite renowned composers have had more effect on music itself than on morals and trends of thought. Few people will dispute the genius of Mozart, for instance, yet although when not writing religious works he expressed and sublimated in musical sound all the trivialities of everyday life, the actual effects of his music were not great, as were those likewise of Haydn, though both these musicians may have had a certain influence on music per se. I have also been asked why, among more recent composers, the names of Elgar and Holst did not figure in my book. But here the reason is a different one. So as not to over-lengthen the volume, it has only been possible to include those composers with the *strongest* influences along particular lines, and not those with weaker influences along similar lines.

PART III
Esoteric Considerations
The Music of the Deva or
Nature-Spirit Evolution

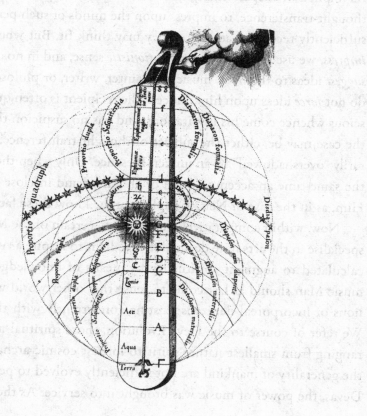

16

Musicians and the Higher Powers

As implied in chapter 5, all high Initiates have the power, by means of thought-transference, to impress upon the minds of such persons as are sufficiently receptive, any ideas they may think fit. But when we write *impress,* we use the word in a *suggestionistic* sense, and in no other. They *suggest* ideas to the poet, musician, painter, writer, or philosopher, they do not *force* ideas upon him. Indeed, the recipient is often quite unconscious whence come his inspirations, and has no suspicion that he is, as the case may be, either the subject of thought transference, or temporarily "overshadowed" by an unseen Presence. Only when the artist is at the same time an accepted pupil of an Adept and in close touch with Him, as in the case of Nelsa Chaplin, can he know these facts.

Now, within comparatively recent years, certain of the Masters who specialise in the arts have deemed it expedient to inspire a type of music calculated to augment spirituality by means of knowledge. Through music Man should at last come to sense that other world with its millions of incorporeal denizens existing concurrently with the physical. We refer of course to the Deva Evolution, those spiritual intelligences ranging from smallest nature-spirit to loftiest cosmic archangel. Since the generality of mankind are not sufficiently evolved to perceive these Devas, the power of music was brought into service. As the melodious utterance of a poet will often convince a sceptic of some truth when no amount of dry argument is of avail, so the melodious sounds of music can achieve a similar, nay, even greater, result. By inspiring composers to convey the vivid life and movements of the Devas, as also their atmosphere and even their music in terms of earthly sound, the Masters are enabling Man to "hear" what as yet he cannot "see." Moreover, by realizing that the Devas exist, Man is approaching that closer relationship between himself and them, which is to constitute such an important evolutionary development of the future.[1]

17

The Occult Constitution of Man

Toward a better comprehension of much that follows, it is necessary at this juncture to study such information as is available regarding Man's subtler bodies, or what have been termed the "sheaths of the soul." Just as psychoanalysis has contributed much to explain the *vagaries* of Man's nature, Theosophy has contributed even more to explain Man's nature itself. Although the spiritualists are proving to the satisfaction of ever-increasing numbers that a human being does not merely consist of a body but also possesses an immortal soul, the Theosophists, or rather the Leaders of the Society, go further, and, as the result of assiduous clairvoyant investigation, have been enabled to give forth specific knowledge regarding the actual constitution of that soul and its relationship to the body and the higher planes of consciousness.

Man's subtler bodies, then, constitute what is known as the aura or auric egg, and are perceptible to the trained clairvoyant of whatever denomination or school of thought; they surround the physical body and interpenetrate one another as well as the physical body itself. In theosophical nomenclature they are termed severally: (1) Etheric body, (2) Astral body, (3) Mental body; but for the purpose of this book they are best tabulated as follows:

1. Physical body or organism, composed of gross matter (sensation body or organism, composed of fine matter)
2. Emotional body or organism, composed of still finer matter
3. Mental body or organism, composed of very fine matter

It will be noted that we have bracketed together the physical—and sensation—bodies, and this because they are so intimately connected that only during an anaesthetic do they become dissociated, whereas the emotional and mental leave the physical in sleep. If a trained seer watches an operation, he can observe the various bodies, *including* the sensation-body, being forced out of the physical by the action of the drug. In the case of a local anaesthetic, however, only a small part of the *sensation-body* is extruded, the other bodies remaining in the physical. The same occurs when one's arm "goes to sleep," for it is possible to force out a part of the sensation-body through pressure; under such conditions the subtle replica of the arm may clairvoyantly be seen projecting from the shoulder; but when the physical-body arm "wakes up," the *sensation-body* arm is reabsorbed, resulting in that feeling of "pins and needles" familiar to all.

It will now have become apparent why we use the term *sensation-body*—i.e., because only when the latter is unified with the physical are sensations possible—in other words, sensation is produced by the conjunction of these two bodies, the one having no feeling independent of the other. But it should be noted that the *sensation-body* is especially significant as regards the present inquiry, for it is on this that the vibrations of music first strike before they affect either the *emotional* or *mental bodies.* Thus, the *sensation-body* is the bridge between the physical and the higher ones, in that it is not possible for comparatively coarse vibrations of sound to affect highly subtilised matter without an intermediary.

As regards the *emotional* and *mental bodies,* the second and third we have enumerated: if a trained clairvoyant looks at the aura of a savage, it reveals an entirely undeveloped *emotional body,* ugly in colouring, small in size, and lacking in all beauty of form. The aura of the moderately evolved man, on the other hand, reveals a larger *emotional body* with purer colouring and more beautiful form. Further, in the aura of the savage there is practically no *mental body* discernible at all, whereas in the average man it varies in size and beauty of colour according to the depth of his intellect and the loftiness of his thoughts. It stands to reason, therefore, that both these bodies are developed in proportion to our emotional and mental lives, and it is for this reason, by the way, that the human aura is an indication of character for those who have the power to see it and to understand the significance of its many hues.*

Nor do these bodies, with the exception of the *sensation-body,* perish with the disintegration of the physical organism; each subtle body, in fact, *is attuned to its corresponding plane of consciousness, and functions independently on that plane when released from the physical envelope,* just as a child functions independently on the physical plane when released from its mother's womb. We may pursue the simile even further: if the foetus is badly nourished, the child will be weak; if its parent is coarse or comes from tainted stock, the child will more than likely be coarse and tainted, and so forth.

But granted that these subtler planes—whether in varying phraseology they be called Heaven, Hell, Purgatory, Kamaloka, Devaloka, or Elysian Fields—granted that they constitute the world of the departed, they bear an even deeper significance in relation to our physical world than the lay mind imagines, And especially is this the case with the *emotional plane.* As the emotions of Man influence the *emotional plane,* so does the *emotional plane* in its turn influence Man's thoughts and feelings. Thus there is a constant interaction between the two. How is it that in certain countries one finds a predominance of certain emotions? The answer is, because the so-called atmosphere or aura—in reality the *emotional plane*—is saturated with those particular emotions.†

---

*The late Dr. Kilner invented a screen by means of which the aura becomes perceptible even to non-clairvoyants.

†During War I, for instance, German Switzerland was very pro-German, while French Switzerland was very pro-Allies: now, it was told to *me* as a curious (?) fact that if an inhabitant of German Switzerland came to stay in French Switzerland, after an astonishingly short time he became as strongly pro-Allies as he had originally been pro-German. And why? Simply because he had moved into that pro-Allies-impregnated aura, i.e., that special part of the *emotional plane* which was located in French Switzerland.

It is instructive to take this cursory view of Man's subtler bodies and their corresponding planes because of the important part that music has played and continues to play in their development. We come to see how each type of music affects one body or the other, and correspondingly, the three domains: the mental, emotional, and material or physical. Thus, in Part IV, we shall see that the quarter-tone of Indian music especially affects the *mental body,* hence the domain of mind, philosophy, metaphysics; the third-tone of ancient Egyptian music especially affected the *emotional body,* hence the domain of the emotions—ritual, music, and occult knowledge; the half-tone of European music especially affects the sensation-physical body—hence the domain of Matter: mechanics, government of men, practicality. Nor is the reason far to seek; the quarter tone is the most subtle division of the note, therefore, it influences the most subtle of the higher bodies; the third tone is a less subtle division, therefore it influences the correspondingly less subtle *emotional body;* the half-tone is the least subtle of all, therefore it influences the physical.*

Yet although we have stated on *what* music *operates,* we have as yet not stated *how;* that is to say, the *modus operandi* considered *esoterically—for* the exoteric modus operandi we have dealt with in chapter 6.

In the Hermetic Philosophy there is a maxim: "As above, so below." Now, speaking in general, music operates in accordance with that Law; but what is actually heard of music is only its physical manifestation consequent upon its vibrations; these pertain to the "below"; or, otherwise expressed, we only perceive the effects of those musical vibrations on the physical plane, but we do not perceive the much further-reaching effects created by that music on the higher planes; *and it is just these,* pertaining to the "above," which influence our various subtler bodies (and hence our characters), because, in addition, they influence those planes themselves. These effects can be perceived by the trained seer, and assume both forms and colours commensurate

*This naturally does not imply that it *exclusively* influences the physical.

with the artistic value and emotions that the music expresses. For instance, the preponderating colour produced by music expressive of devotion, is blue—that being the colour of Devotion on the higher planes—and, consequently, in the *emotional body*. Hence, if the seer looks at the aura of even a fairly devotional person, he will find in it this colour. Now, as like attracts like, especially on the super-physical planes, the blue produced by that devotional music will tend to increase the blue in the aura of that particular person, and so to increase the attribute of Devotion. It is the same with all other emotions and their corresponding colours. But the following point should be specially noted: where a man is entirely lacking in a particular quality, and hence in its corresponding colour, then in that particular respect the subtler manifestation of music cannot affect him. Were it otherwise, the least evolved souls would develop with an astonishing rapidity, and in the large cities where there are concert halls and opera houses, squalor and sordidness would be nonexistent. That such is not the case, we are all too sadly aware. Nonetheless, even the most undisciplined characters are susceptible to the beneficial influence, however slight, of such music as they actually hear, and for this reason even barrel-organs served a useful purpose in the slums.

There is, however, one very important point we have still to add, namely, that the subtler effects of *played* music, i.e., the colours and forms produced on the *emotional plane,* endure for some time after the actual sounds have died away. In other words, though the music itself is no longer heard, the emotional content of that music is operative for a varying while within a certain radius around the spot where it was played. To give a simile, if an inadequate one: when we throw a pebble into a pond, though the pebble itself is small, the rings it produces on the surface of the water are large. If there be a bit of straw floating a considerable distance from the spot where the pebble sank, after an appreciable space of time that bit of straw will be agitated by one of those rings. Now, the same law on a much larger scale obtains in connection with the subtler effects of music. Although the Albert Hall itself—wherein we will suppose a certain work is being performed—occupies a comparatively small amount of space, the colours and forms created by that work on the *emotional plane* extend for some distance around. It is for this reason that *it is unnecessary for a person to be within earshot of music in order to benefit, at any rate to some extent, by its effects.* Nor must we forget the durability of those effects. Presuming a man lives in an outlying suburb but comes into London daily for business purposes, although he lives and sleeps outside the subtler influences of that music, he comes under them every day during business hours.

To summarise: the art of music, as will be gathered from all the foregoing, is operative in two ways—grossly and subtly; on the physical plane "heard strains" by their charm possess the power to "soothe the savage breast," while "unheard strains" possess hidden powers of a "telepathic" nature, which affect our subtler bodies directly or through the "emotional atmosphere," and so educate the "soul."

But an important objection may here arise. Let us again suppose there is a concert at some hall, and that a hundred yards away music of an entirely different kind is being played at a cinema: is not the effect produced in the unseen planes one of discordant chaos? And yet we answer: not so—for in the unseen planes there are other dimensions of space[1] to be taken into account—and also the fact that one type of vibration does not interfere with another type, any more than the vibrations of the sunlight interfere with those of the hidden rays of wireless telegraphy. Only if two concerts took place within earshot and actually produced discord on the physical plane would that discord be reproduced on the unseen planes—not otherwise.

There is, however, still the effect on our subtler bodies to be considered: the effect of two or more musical performances *not* within earshot. In this case, each person will, in accordance with our former statement, be affected by that quality to which he is most capable of responding. For example, let us suppose there is a man living midway between two concert halls, and that in the one a fugue of Bach is being, or has been, performed, while in the other a violinist is, or has been, playing the second movement of Mendelssohn's *Violin Concerto.* If the man in question has much yellow in his aura—yellow being the colour of intellect—then the yellow produced by Bach's music* will increase it, for, as we have said, like attracts like. And let us suppose that he is an abnormal man without a grain of sympathy in his character, and consequently not a trace of apple-green—the corresponding colour—in his aura, then he will be impervious to the influence of Mendelssohn's music. Should he, on the other hand, possess a certain degree of this attribute, then he will derive benefit from both concerts, the one acting on his *emotional body,* the other on his *mental.* Needless to say, this principle is susceptible to countless variations, the human aura being composed of a variety of colours corresponding to a man's many attributes. Thus several different influences may be brought to bear on the *emotional body* alone at one and the same time.

*See *ante.*

18

César Franck, the Bridge between the Humans and the Devas

Although César Franck was born nearly twenty years later than Berlioz, he was the father of that French school of composers that was destined to introduce quite a new element in musical *content,* if not altogether in form. For Berlioz, with all his ingenuity, must be regarded as an experimentalist; he was never able to introduce into his music that subtle ingredient, which influences character and moulds morals; he influenced music itself, and prepared the way for the genius of Wagner, and to some extent for Franck.

The latter "first saw the light of day," to use an expression characteristic of his era, at Liège in 1822; and it is not without significance that the first Deva-exponent should be one of the most touching and beautiful characters in the annals of musical biography. His portrait is familiar to all music-lovers, but only those who have read M. Vincent d'Indy's *study* relating to him will obtain a glimpse of the soul of this remarkable man. Even those who met him in life—casually, that is to say—never suspected the genius that lay hidden in the heart of that strange little figure, so often to be seen hurrying along, "invariably absent-minded and making grimaces, running rather than walking," and "dressed in an overcoat a size too large, and trousers a size too short . . ." Nevertheless, that little figure whose face was as quaintly adorned—(he had thick, grey side whiskers but a clean-shaven mouth and chin)—as the rest of his person, radiated a love so warm and selfless "that his pupils not only cared for him as a father, but were attached to each other in and through him." Yet though he merited so much, his external life was one of unutterable drudgery.[1] From morning to night, apart from those he gave to his inner circle of disciples, he was obliged to give lessons to none-too-intelligent amateurs, and what is more, to contend with the stupid myopia of jealous academic conservatoire professors. It was characteristic of his noble nature, however, that far from bearing Fate or *them* any ill-will, he seemed to be oblivious of their evil intentions. With all his literary interests and intellectual pursuits there was something so intrinsically naive, trusting and childlike in his heart, that to disbelieve in the goodness of humanity, even in the face of evidence to the contrary, was impossible. No wonder that César Franck proved a fit instrument in the hands of the Higher Powers, and that the Masters could so mould his inspirational faculties that he could receive the higher Deva message, either through Them, or in certain conditions direct from the Devas Themselves.

Those who, while in the body, can clairvoyantly see the Devas, or else bring back the memory of Them after super-conscious trances, know that one of the chief Deva characteristics is Love; but, of course, this attribute varies with the spiritual altitude of the Devas in question—in the little nature-spirit it is existent but to a correspondingly lesser degree. That a tone-poet who was in close touch with the higher type of Deva should manifest this same love was both natural and significant. Yet, unless to begin with he had possessed a measure of that beautiful attribute in his soul, it would not have been possible for either Adept or Deva to inspire him. But apart from Franck's love-nature, there are other signs that he was closely in touch with the Deva-evolution. He was a master of that form of improvisation, which Initiates know to be the Devic type; moreover, his achievements in this direction were perhaps even more inspired than his written work;

and this lends much weight to our contention. "For César Franck had, or rather *was*, the genius of improvisation." In the "dusk of the organ-loft" in that church of St. Clotilde, where he held the post of organist, every Sunday and feast-day he would "pour out his soul" in wonderful fantasias, "which were often far more lofty than many skillfully elaborated compositions." And it is just this spontaneity, thus finding expression, which is so evidential of the Deva-inspired, or the Deva-overshadowed man. Franck was an ardent believer, and we read that every Sunday during Mass "he would leave the organ-loft, and, kneeling in a corner of the gallery, prostrate himself in fervent adoration before the Almighty Presence at the altar." This simple act of faith on his part is full of meaning to those who, gifted with seership, can perceive the radiant-coloured Devas as they fill a church, having been evoked by means of that ancient piece of Ceremonial Magic. It was then, no doubt, that César Franck came into even closer touch with those "Shining Ones" whose very speech he so often endeavoured to reproduce in earthly music; it was then that "he assuredly foresaw and conceived the sublime melodies, which afterwards formed the groundwork of *The Beatitudes.*"[2]

César Franck lived to be sixty-eight years of age. With a life remarkable for its energy and freedom from disease, he was the first composer, as we shall presently see, whose mission it was to break down disease in the lives of others. He died on November 8, 1890, and his journey to the grave was as free from all outward display as had been his life. Not one representative of the Conservatoire where he had taught for so long came to his funeral, not one eminent professor or official from the Ministry or the Department of Fine Arts. Every person of worldly eminence who received an invitation excused himself—there was, in fact, a strange epidemic of brief but debilitating indisposition, which attacked all the great musical professors of Paris just around November 8 of that year! And so "only the Master's numerous pupils, his friends, and the musicians whom his untiring kindness had won over to him" appeared at his graveside. It was an all the more poetical ending to an inwardly poetical life, and the final touch of poetry was added when

M. Chabrier delivered that valedictory oration, which deserves to be recorded in many books. It ended

> Farewell, Master, and take our thanks, for you have done well. In you we salute one of the greatest artists of the century, and also the incomparable teacher whose wonderful work has produced a whole generation of forceful musicians, believers and thinkers, armed at all points for hard-fought and prolonged conflicts. We salute, also, the upright and just man, so humane, so distinguished, whose counsels were sure, as his words were kind. Farewell. . . .

An examination of César Franck's music reveals to us two distinct elements, the human and the ethereal. The second movement of the *Violin Sonata* affords an instance of the expression of the former, the noted *cantilene* in the *Pianoforte Quintet* affords an instance of the expression of the latter. It is owing to the combination of these two phases that we have designated Franck a bridge between the human evolution and the Deva; he expresses the emotions of both and so co-ordinates the mortal with the celestial. As Mr. Gustave Devepas writes:

> César Franck's music makes us neither beast nor angel. Keeping a steady balance, as far removed from materialistic coarseness, as from the hallucinations of a doubtful mysticism, it accepts humanity with all its positive joys and sorrows, and uplifts it, without dizziness, to peace and serenity, by revealing the sense of the Divine. Thus it tends to contemplation rather than to ecstasy. The hearer who abandons himself with docility to its beneficent influence will recover from the superficial agitation at *the centre of the soul,* and, with all that is best within himself, will return to the attraction of the *supremely desirable,* which is at the same time the *supremely intelligible.* Without ceasing to be human he will find himself nearer to God. This music, which is truly as much *the sister of prayer as of poetry,* does not weaken or enervate us, but rather *restores to the soul,*

now led back to its first source, the grateful waters of emotion, of light, of impulse; it leads back to heaven and to the city of rest.

And to this M. Vincent d'Indy adds: "In a word, it leads us from egoism to love . . . from the world to the soul, from the soul to God."[3]

This latter reflection is deeply significant. Egoism is the cause of most of the troubles which fret the mind of Man. A large variety, even of physical maladies, are both engendered and aggravated by self-centredness; consequently many of those schools of healing, which tend to "lift people out of themselves" have proved so efficacious. Indeed it was one of the Masters who inspired that particular type of metaphysics, which developed into Higher Thought, Christian Science, and similar movements. What César Franck achieved through the agency of music, these movements sought to achieve through metaphysical argument. By "revealing a sense of the divine," and by leading Man "back to heaven," Franck led him away from his small personal self and gave him a glimpse of his Higher Self in which there is neither sorrow nor disease. In Franck's music there is truly the healing balm of that seraphic love, which harmonises all the subtler bodies, and tends to bring them into alignment. As darkness and the sunlight cannot exist in one and the same place, neither can sorrow and disease exist where shines the joy- and health-giving Love of the Angelic Hosts.

To enter into an elaborate analysis of Franck's music, however interesting to the musician, would serve no purpose as regards this book. Suffice it to say that through the ethereality, "nobility and expressive value of his melodic phrase, and the originality of his harmonic combinations,"* he contrived to reproduce some of the Deva-music of the higher planes for the benefit of earthly ears. One result of his achievement was that diffusion of practical mysticism throughout Europe that began toward the end of last century. Mankind in general is averse to accepting anything new, not only is the objective mind in resistance to it, but still more the subconscious. It was this resistance in the subconscious

---

*Vincent d'Indy's phrases

that César Franck was instrumental in breaking down; he helped to insinuate into it those very ideas, which later on, so many people came to accept. Since his advent, the science of healing with the aid of "Nature's finer forces" has vastly increased. Verily, as M. Chabrier said when bidding him that final good-bye, *he had done well,* for to inspire those measures whereby the burden of sorrow and disease may be lifted from the souls and bodies of a suffering humanity is to have accomplished a great work that merits our undying gratitude.

And yet M. Chabrier thus eulogized César Franck without knowing the whole truth. Franck was an Initiate, albeit without clairvoyance. Special Devas under the guidance of the Adept Koot Hoomi, who was his Master, poured down inspiration through his subtle bodies, thereby creating an exquisite chord on the higher planes, combining their individual notes with those of the Adept and His unwitting pupil on earth.

When he returns to the world of men, it will be with those powers characteristic of the advanced Initiate: the ability to see, to hear, and to heal by super-physical means.

19
Grieg, Tchaikovsky, and Delius

As Franck was an intermediary between the higher Devas and humanity, Edvard Grieg was an intermediary between the little nature-spirit and humanity. Although his creations were in many respects charming and individual, they did not reach the altitude attained by the Belgian composer. Nor, in view of what we have just written, could this be demanded: the nature-spirits are quaint little entities whose relationship to even the lesser Devas merely resembles that of our domestic animals to *us,* and, therefore, to expect either great loftiness or profundity from their musical interpreter—and their *first* at that—would be to expect the impossible.

That Grieg should be born in Scandinavia is in itself significant; for there, as in Ireland, Scotland, and Wales, the nature-spirits are nearer to humanity than in countries where the towns pollute the physical atmosphere with their smoke-belching chimneys, and the spiritual atmosphere with their materialism and acquisitiveness. Thus, in residing in Norway, Grieg lived in close touch with the untarnished soul of nature. Also, the folk song of that country, which exercised such a marked influence on his work, was already to some extent expressive of the nature-spirit element. As the writer in *Grove's Dictionary* remarks: "Grieg's music carries the fragrance of his native pinewoods into the concert room." Yes, and in the last number of the *Peer Gynt Suite,* he also carries a suggestion of dancing gnomes.

It is not our intention, however, to expatiate at any length on the Norwegian composer, for his influence on mankind was not a pronounced, though at the time in some respects a very necessary one: he inserted the thin end of the wedge that was eventually to widen the crevice through which mankind should obtain a larger view over the nature-spirit world. It was he who paved the way for Frederick Delius, Claude-Achille Debussy, Stravinsky, and others, and finally for Scriabin: the greatest Deva-exponent who has so far appeared in the field of art.

Nevertheless, Grieg was not entirely alone in his unconscious endeavours to span the chasm between the two worlds; three years before his birth[1]* another composer—destined to reap an astonishing popularity—was born at Kamsko-Votinsk, in Russia: Pyotr Ilyich Tchaikovsky. And although it must be admitted that a very large proportion of Tchaikovsky's work was almost too obviously human, seeing that at times he did undoubtedly write nature-music, he, too, must be accepted as an intermediary. He may, owing to his glaring unsubtleties, be regarded by the genuine and more pronounced nature-spirit exponents as a musical vulgarian, but their attitude does not alter the facts. That attitude, indeed, is perfectly comprehensible; for one of the chief characteristics of nature-music is its subtlety, and, therefore, to composers like Ravel and Debussy, in whom this virtue is very pronounced, "the most un-Russian of all the Russians," as Ravel called him, could not be expected to appeal; they had outgrown his immature efforts, which no doubt savoured to them of the nursery. If, however, despite their censure, we care to examine parts of Tchaikovsky's music, we detect a certain primitive quaintness not unlike that of Grieg, though by this we mean the spirit of Grieg's work and not the form. But even so this quaintness to be found in both composers is more *reminiscent* of nature-music, than actually *like* it, judging from how it sounds to clair-audient ears. The work that Grieg and Tchaikovsky accomplished was

---

*Viz., in 1843

more to draw attention to the existence of the nature-spirit music by portraying what they *thought* it was like than by reproducing it *actually*. For this the time was not ripe, seeing that the knowledge of the Deva-evolution was not intended for the world until after Wagner's influence had spread to a certain extent.

But apart from this, it was not possible that music itself should undergo a sudden transformation at the hands of its exponents. For Grieg or Tchaikovsky to have conceived of an entirely new music would have been contrary to the laws that govern inspirational receptivity. However much an Adept or Deva might wish to impress a *totally* and consistently novel combination of ideas upon one of His "mediums," the latter would be incapable of receiving it; for one thing, it would be contrary to all his previous musical notions, for another, he would not have the necessary technique at his disposal to transmit it. Therefore, musical evolution, just as every other kind of evolution, must be a gradual process, in view both of its composers and its listeners. Hitherto, even the most advanced Deva-exponents have only been able to "bring through" a small portion of that music, and that is why the "hyper-moderns" sound to us so discordant: they have assimilated some of the discords, but have not learnt how to resolve them. Moreover, they have still to "bring through" the melodic side of the Deva-music; for, not having as yet sensed this, many of them, in their endeavours to avoid the obvious, banish melody from their compositions altogether. It should also be stated that the necessary instruments for the perfect interpretation of this music have yet to be invented.

Thus, in reviewing the whole trend of that art, which had its first tentative beginnings with Grieg and Tchaikovsky, all the foregoing must be taken into consideration.

The next progressive step from the human to the Deva music is to be found in the works of Frederick Delius: for he has undoubtedly contacted much of the *atmosphere* of the nature-spirit evolution. If we compare his art with that of his predecessors, we find it appreciably softer, more mellow, and more subtle; it is also essentially refined. Delius, like all other individualists, developed his style through a selective process—he assimilated certain phases of Grieg, of Debussy, and Wagner, and made them his own. He is the poet of *atmosphere,* of the peace-fragranced spirit of the woods, of the freedom of the "cloud-kissing hill," and of the hazy sun-bathed landscape. The folk song has also played its part in his development, as it did in that of Grieg, for in the folk song he found that closer communion with Nature, which aided his creativeness.

20
Debussy and Ravel

When Beethoven wrote his *Pastoral Symphony,* although he may have portrayed the feelings of humans *towards* Nature, he never echoed the music of Nature itself—for, after all, the call of one irrepressible cuckoo does not make a rural poem, nor does a tympani roll—which was intended to depict a thunderstorm. The introduction of these flagrant insignia of Nature, in fact, merely suggest the naive; they conjure up a child with a pencil whose one idea of drawing a man is to give him a beard. But the propitious time for Nature-music had not arrived, and, even so, Beethoven could never have composed it: he lacked the essential subtlety.

Those who listen to the piping of the birds, to the murmur of the breeze among the foliage, to the laughter of the pebble-studded stream, and try to catch their elusive harmonies, must realise that the keynote of Nature's music is its extreme subtlety. All is enchantingly indefinite, between the notes, varied, yet in a sense charmingly monotonous. If the birds were actually to sing tunes, they would pall upon us like the cuckoo and destroy all their poetry—tunes soon become commonplace—but never the song of the thrush or blackbird; it always eludes us, and that is why we love it.

If one thinks of the opening phrase of Debussy's *L'Après-midi d'un Faune,* this same subtlety is noticeable; all is subdued, delicate, nebulous—for Debussy was the first composer to turn entirely from the human and write Nature-music pure and simple. It was his mission to begin at the first rung of the Devic evolutionary ladder, and echo the music of the gnomes and fairies, the spirits of the water, and the spirits of the clouds. Hence, he was instinctively compelled to write tone-poems bearing such titles as *Nuages, La Mer, Jardins sous la Pluie, Reflets dans l'eau,* and so forth. It is true that he stepped into fame with an opera composed to Maeterlinck's *Pelléas et Mélisande,* but it was the remoteness of this play, which attracted him, not its humanity. Hence, the result was an anomaly: nature-spirit music to a drama of human jealousy is out of place, and that is why his opera is not altogether satisfying; it is too attenuated and diaphanous, and there comes a moment when one begins to feel that it is too long. But then nature-spirit music is not suited to opera at all, unless the subject be a fairytale or culled from mythology; for the nature-spirits know no passions nor sorrows, nor have they any moral sense as we understand it; joie de vivre is their most prominent characteristic. They sing, they dance, they bathe in the sun or moonbeams, they love to mould the clouds into countless different shapes, they love to play pranks and transform themselves into various semblances, just as children love to "dress up." In fact, they are very similar to children, and have a special partiality for them, and will often play with those who are psychically disposed. The parental wiseacres, of course, when their offspring relate of the games they have had with fairies, think that it is all imagination; but this is not so, in that the young are very often gifted with psychic vision, though they as often lose their gifts when they grow up. Being told that it is all nonsense, they suppress those natural faculties, which, in consequence, atrophy.

We need not go into elaborate details relative to Debussy's work; it has sufficed to show its similitude to the subtle music of Nature, yet only those who possess clairaudience will realize *how* great that similitude. For what may be heard with the physical ear—the sighing of the breeze, the laughter of the brook—is but the outer manifestation of Nature's minstrelsy; there is an inner song made by every movement of the leaves, of the butterflies' wings, of even the flower petals as they open to the kiss of the sun. And it is this that Debussy has reproduced as far as it has been possible with our present-day instruments.

Nevertheless, without great elaboration, a word should be said about his remarkable harmonic inventiveness: for with his advent an almost entirely new world of harmony was revealed to us. It was not, however, a greatly discordant world despite its novelty—with the exception of such pieces as *La Cathédrale Engloutie*—Debussy contrived to be new without being intensely harsh; his discords were more subtle than ear-splitting. They may have fallen strangely on the aural senses of 1902, when *Pelléas* was first produced, but they cannot compare in actual harshness with those of Schönberg or Bartok. The reason is that (1) Debussy was concerned with depicting the naturespirit music of the earth-plane, which, being near to us, is more familiar than that of the remoter planes—remoter only in a sense, of course, since they interpenetrate the physical; and (2) that he reproduced much more of that music in its entirety than have the later composers reproduced of the music of the Emotional Plane. In a word, his music is more complete than that of his followers. But nonetheless, it has its limitations, as Debussy himself was the first to admit. "I have come to the end of my tether," he once said in effect to the author of this book. "My message is not an extended one; I seem to have exhausted its possibilities and can't branch out in other directions." Did he perhaps feel intuitively that his life was drawing to a close? It may be so, for he said this just before he developed the malady that resulted in his death.

But he was not left without an heir—musically speaking—to elaborate his mission and widen his influence. This is not to say that Maurice Ravel is a "copy" of Debussy, but rather a variation of him. Ravel, in fact, constitutes the bridge between the music of the nature-spirits and that of the lesser Devas—those who inhabit the Emotional Plane; for he oscillates, as it were, between the unseen denizens of the physical and those of that higher Plane; he is a necessary step to Scriabin's message. With Ravel the discordant element is more pronounced than with his predecessor; at the same time his form is more elaborate, as witness the *Trio for Piano, Violin, and Cello*. He also took upon himself—unconsciously, no doubt—that high mission of showing the beautiful in the ugly, not relative to the human realm as did Moussorgsky (see chapter 23), but to the realm of Nature. For it must be admitted that there is a wealth of beauty in the ugly side of Nature when we look upon it in its completeness; *Le Gibet* is one of the most characteristic pieces in this field of endeavour, though, in order to assimilate its message, we must listen to it with our feelings, so to say, and not with our mind.

Like Debussy, Ravel embarked on an opera with a very human subject: the music of *L'Heure Espagnole* is nonhuman nevertheless, and is even more of an anomaly than that of *Pelléas*. If its plot bears any resemblance whatever to the nature-spirit world, it is solely in that complete absence of conventional moral sense, which its characters exhibit; in all other respects there is none. The Higher Powers, however, do not dictate to their "mediums" the choice of *libretti;* they are content to inspire the music, though, of course, had Ravel been a conscious occultist, or like Wagner or Scriabin aiming at some philosophical message, he would have coordinated the two. As it is, his intuition only at times played him false, seeing that for the most part it guided him to select apt superscriptions for the majority of his pieces. Only a nature-spirit tone-poet would think of such a title as *Undines,* and only a nature-lover would hit on the fantastic idea of setting natural history to music.

Since Debussy and Ravel have spread abroad their influence, a perceptible change in the attitude towards the "Unseen" has taken place. Popular magazines print articles dealing with the subject of Fairies as possible objective realities and not merely as figments of the imagination; the interest in folklore has widely increased, savants having published books on the folklore of the various countries. Spiritism is obtaining an ever greater hold on the nation. Moreover, the number of people with psychic perception is increasing, and instead of being scoffed at as visionaries, their assertions are taken with a degree of seriousness, which formerly would not have been accorded them. In a word, the chasm between the seen and the unseen is growing ever narrower.

21

Scriabin, a Deva-Exponent

It is not altogether strange that Scriabin's early compositions should have been intensely Chopinesque in character, for refinement and subtlety are closely allied. Thus, his predilection for the idiom of Chopin was based on psychological reasons rather than on musical ones; from an ultra-refinement, and hence subtilising of the human element, Scriabin passed into the non-human, and so ultimately became the greatest exponent of Deva-music who so far has been born. He was also the first Russian composer who combined a theoretical knowledge of occultism with the tonal art. Scriabin knew that he had a spiritual message to convey to the world, and that through music it could be given; he did not believe in *l'art pour l'art;* such a conception failed to appeal to his mystic temperament; he wanted to benefit the human race, and it was this aspiration, which impelled him to confess that the day on which his *chef de oeuvre* could be produced, would be the happiest in his life.

This *chef de oeuvre* was to be called a *Misterium,* and at its perfecting Scriabin aimed during the last fifteen years of his all-too-short existence on earth. Not only was it calculated to express the composer's spiritual ideas, but to have an actually spiritualising effect on its listeners. Further, "it was to have been delivered in the form of a service that would consist of a combined and simultaneous appeal to the senses by all the arts"[1]—a magnificent scheme, indeed, if realizable—but unfortunately death overtook the composer before its completion. Did the Powers of Evil begin to "walk in awe of this mortal" and to fear his influence, as M. Montagu-Nathan suggests, or was it that the time was not ripe for so exalted a revelation? Certainly it seems strange that all the efforts of the doctors to prevent a carbuncle from proving fatal should be unavailing. And yet occult information has solved for us this tragic enigma. Unlike Franck, Scriabin was not a trained Initiate working under the supervision of a Master; and hence in contacting the Devas of the higher planes, he subjected his delicate physical vehicle to such a strain that he laid himself open to the attacks of the Dark Forces. Not being clairvoyant and possessed of the necessary knowledge, he was unable to keep them at bay. Moreover, as the powers of those Devas who had inspired him were restricted to their own planes, they were impotent to protect him. Thus, he died at forty-three years of age with his greatest work unaccomplished.

In 1910, *Prometheus* or the *Poem of Fire* was completed, and it is undoubtedly the most mature of the composer's works. Scriabin had already discovered that harmonic system which is preeminently Devic in character, and in this work he put it to the fullest use. The effect is one of almost continuous *false relation,* i.e. "the occurrence of chromatic contradiction in different parts" played simultaneously. And yet only through this device, which caused the pedagogues of an earlier period to shudder with righteous indignation, is it possible to obtain that sense of "between the notes," which is essential to the portrayal of Deva-music. True, Mr. Foulds in his *World Requiem* attempted to simulate that music with the employment of quarter-tones, but not altogether successfully, since the effect rather gave rise to the idea that the orchestra was playing out of tune. But then, as Initiates who can see into the future have pointed out, special instruments are necessary for quarter-tone effects, and the day has not yet arrived for their invention. In the meantime, the possibilities of *false relation* are far from being exhausted, as witness the free use of it made by every noteworthy composer of the present day.

The Devic quality of Scriabin's music, however, is not only to be traced in his harmonic scheme, but in that exuberance and ecstasy that colour nearly the whole of his *Prometheus* score. It is an entirely different type of ecstatic element from that produced by Wagner: all sense of the obvious and the diatonic is banished, and with it all sense of the human. It exhales an intense loveliness, but not an earthly loveliness; it reaches a climax expressive of unutterable grandeur, but it is a grandeur incomparable with anything we have seen or experienced on earth. It is the grandeur of mighty Beings, flashing forth Their unimaginable colours and filling the vast expanses with Their song. It was because Scriabin was inspired so forcibly to express the Deva-evolution that he felt the necessity for employing the "keyboard of light" in conjunction with the orchestra; his intense predilection for trills arose from the same cause. Those endowed with a sufficiently high type of clairvoyance to see the Devas on the more rarefied planes tell us that they scintillate with the most superb colours. The colours of earth, with the exception of those produced by fire or those in the sunset, are dead; but on the higher planes all are vibrant and alive. Moreover, colour, music, perfume, are all synthesised and not apportioned to different senses as in the material world. Thus, when Scriabin aimed at a synthesis of all the arts, he was attempting to demonstrate that Law of Correspondences: "as above, so below."

It should be remembered that Scriabin was in touch with a higher stage of the Deva-evolution than was Debussy. Exquisite as are the latter's compositions they do not approach either the ecstasy or the grandeur expressed by those of Scriabin. His whole range was a more extended one, but as he never attempted to synthesise the Devic and the human elements, his music seldom touches the heart: there is something impersonal about it, with all its ecstasy. Yet it does not leave us cold; on the contrary, it stirs us vitally, but it awakens emotions that are less translatable into words than those evoked by any previous composer. Could it be otherwise, seeing that as yet the majority of us do not even dimly understand that vast evolutionary scheme of which it relates?

22

The Ultra-Discordants and Their Effects

It is a fact that intense and continued passional emotions, especially mob emotions, create a variety of thought-forms in the lower of the unseen planes, and that these thought-forms endure for a number of years, until destroyed by some specific agency. Looked at clairvoyantly, they often appear as a dense miasmic vapour with tentacles reaching out in all directions, ready at any moment to pounce on the unwary and inject their poison into their emotional organism.

In the Middle Ages these *thought-forms* were, in part, responsible for the many and varied manifestations of cruelty mentioned in the chronicles of that period. That they obsessed some of the inquisitors, for instance, we have reason to believe. After the Reformation, these thought-forms played their part in inciting the various sects to persecute one another and resort to violent measures in order to suppress so-called heresy. At a still later period they inspired the cruelty and bloodshed coincident with the French Revolution. Indeed, if we study world history we shall find that at every period, somewhere or other, acts of violence and cruelty have been perpetrated. For these thought-forms merely shift their field of action from one people, one country to another: the focus for their attack being always some emotional upheaval. It must be understood, however, that thought-forms *in them-*

selves are not possessed of any great motive force, but that they attract the Powers of Evil and their agents, who utilise them for their own purposes; thus humanity itself, by wrong thinking, forges the weapons that those Powers may wield to its own detriment.

Now it should be noted that nearly all the music we have hitherto examined in this inquiry has been educative, but *not* destructive. The specific type of music essential to the destruction of these undesirable obsessing thought-forms only began to come into existence around 1906: it is the music of the ultra-discordant type. For it is an occult musical fact that discord (used in its moral sense) can alone be destroyed *by* discord, the reason for this being that the vibrations of intrinsically beautiful music are too rarefied to touch the comparatively coarse vibrations of all that pertains to a much lower plane. No more than a mass of slime in a stagnant pool can be affected by the blue haze of a summer's morn, can those turgid thought-forms be affected by the strains of purely concordant music.

Of course the question may here be asked: "Why did not the Higher Powers inspire the essential species of music centuries ago? Surely, if discord is all that was needed, it could have been 'put through' immediately after, say, the Gladiatorial Games" (see chapter 30). But the answer to this is that mere discord in itself will not produce the desired result: it must perforce be a special type of discord, which can only be engendered by the musical material at our disposal in this the twentieth century. The dissonances produced by "a few sorry pipes" would have been quite powerless to destroy those mighty thought-forms: one might as well attempt to destroy the effluvia of a cesspool by lighting a joss-stick over it.

Thus, the work of destroying them was to a certain extent allotted to Stravinsky, but more particularly to Schönberg and one or two of his followers to whom some wags have referred to as "the excrutiationists" or "the boys of the sour chords!" And yet however much the works of these ultra-discordant composers may jar the nerves of music-lovers who prefer more pleasant examples of the tonal art, they were needed, esoterically speaking, not only for the purpose already mentioned, but also to break down that conventionality that was one of the by-effects of Handel's music. Only dissonances possess the power to alter the hard outlines of the *mental bodies* of pharisaical or conventional people, and so render them more pliant and receptive to new ideas.

Nevertheless, there is another side to the picture: the ultra-discordants—though they are pleased to say that there is no such thing as a discord—have had an undesirable effect on music itself, or perhaps better said, on composers. For although this type of music is no longer needed, it has become the fashion to write it, and even to label all non-ultra-discordant contemporary music as "romantic"—a catchword that has become one of abuse. Admittedly a certain proportion of discords is essential to all high art, but it is only the inspired composer who senses how to resolve them rightly. Actually the cacophonous school is a *perversion* of Deva-music of one kind, and would be real Deva-music if its votaries possessed the ability to resolve their discords in the true Devic way. As for musical fashions, they have come and gone, and it is only those really creative composers who withstood their influence, whose works have lived; as witness those of Brahms. Had he in his later years wanted to "bring himself up to date," he might have adopted some of the Wagnerian methods; but he chose to remain true to himself, with the result that the musical public has remained true to *him*. Yet that spate of composers who wrote in the Wagnerian style, minus Wagner's genius, have all been forgotten save Bruckner, who can hardly be regarded as a great master.

The Hierarchy has intimated that the ultra-dissonant phase of music will not endure, and it was never intended that it should.

23

Moussorgsky and the Sublimation of Ugliness

Modeste Petrovich Moussorgsky was born in 1839 and died in 1881. He was a man who held very distinct views, and pronounced the laudable dictum that "musicians should not base their art on the laws of the past, but on the needs of the future."[1] And although he was acquainted with those laws, he composed as he felt: "unhampered by the traditions which become second nature to the schooled musician."[2] His mode of life seems to have been likewise unhampered by the traditions of conduct, for it was so unregulated that he died from the results of sheer dissipation, having first alienated himself on that account from all his friends. Yet, as we shall see, his character and mode of life were intimately connected with his mission; he was the Baudelaire of music, destined to poeticalise the ugly and the morbid; he was equally the Zola of music, portraying the sordid aspects of life.

Those who have had the patience to follow our inquiry thus far will need no detailed analysis of Moussorgsky's art to realise the truth of what has just been stated; they have but to listen to some of his strange songs, and to parts of *Boris Godunov*. But, even so, they may not realise the full significance from a spiritual evolutionary point

133

of view of thus portraying squalor and sordidness in music. If, however, we imagine for a moment the consciousness of the perfected
Man, we must realise that one of the factors in that consciousness is
the power to see beauty in everything. As he who can only love his
friends and kindred has not acquired the true unconditional Love-
consciousness expressed in the maxim, "Love thy neighbour as thy-
self," so he who can only perceive beauty in the *obviously* beautiful
has not attained the *true* perception of Beauty. The soul that would
evolve must evolve in all directions, and in order to reach the highest, must not shirk the lowest; he must, in the proverbial phrase, "go
through hell to find heaven." It was this spiritually educative aspect
of Moussorgsky's music that inspired that school of painters whose
métier is the sublimation of ugliness. Since Gauguin and Van Gogh,
to mention only two, appeared in the field, sombre coloured, the por-
traiture of ugly women, the representation of the so-called coarse, of
the smoke-begrimed and squalid side of life: all these have become the
subject-matter of pictorial art.

But Moussorgsky's music had yet other effects. By bringing home
to the hearts of the Russian people the squalor and misery of their existence, and at the same time with his discords breaking down conventional thinking, he ultimately helped to arouse that hatred of bondage
that resulted in the Revolution. To the more evolved soul, including
that of the artist and the writer, he showed the beauty in squalor; to the
"man in the street" he showed the misery of it, and implanted within
him the longing to be free.

We are aware that a seeming paradox is here involved, but one need
only turn to the Bible to perceive that all spiritual science is replete with
paradox:* it cannot be otherwise while human beings are at varying
stages of evolution. The same agent that gives life to one gives death to
another: does not the sun spell life to the flowers and death to noisome
germs? And so again we see the Law of Correspondences: as in Music,
so in Life.

---

*For instance, "He who would save his life must lose it."

Nevertheless, to Moussorgsky alone we must not look for those causes that brought about the Revolution: other notable Russian composers added their quota. If we examine the characteristics of nearly all Russian music, we find insistence of rhythm one of the most pronounced. Now very marked rhythm, by reason of its power to "rouse up," to energise, gives to man *enthusiasm*, spirit, courage, audacity. Alone to exhibit the sordidness of life, as Moussorgsky did, would not have eventuated in a revolution; we may draw a man's attention to the misery of his surroundings, but unless by one means or another we can fire him with enthusiasm and daring, nothing practical is achieved. The folk-dance music had already done much to imbue the Russians with boldness and patriotism, but it was the ballet, with all its enthusiasm-creating rhythms and tone-colour, that finally put the torch to a long smoldering fire and endowed, at any rate, the leaders of the revolution with the essentials to set it in motion.

24
Popular Music and Its Various Effects

ENGLISH "BALLADS"

The pieces of music, which come under the above heading, are not to be confounded with such classical specimens as "Chevy Chase" or "Adam Bell": indeed, strictly speaking, they are not ballads at all, they are simply songs, and of a most banal and sentimental nature. Nevertheless, they had their uses during that Victorian Age in which they played so large a part. With their sloppy sentimentality, they counteracted the hardness of the Victorian people, and even, strange though it may sound, the hardness of the Victorian furniture. At a period when everything was subservient to Duty, when awe and reverence had sunk into the blood and bones of the nation, they inspired a modicum of a particular kind of sympathy. It was that kind, which, as a great concession, permitted a slight note of frivolity in otherwise austere surroundings; that kind, which allowed children to play a game on Sundays, provided it was in some way connected with religion. This slight concession, transferred to the plane of furniture, was answerable for the Japanese fans, the wax flowers, and other knick-knacks.

The ballads, however, have now been ousted from the public taste by creations of a much higher class, such as those of Roger Quilter, who possessed a genius for true songwriting, and by those of other English composers. It may be added that all songs, which are *genuine* songs and not a species of *recitative* superimposed upon an accompaniment, tend to inspire sympathy, give poise and balance, and sustain the gentler side of life. In the case of Roger Quilter's works, by their touch of the Devic element they arouse sympathy and love for the beauties of Nature.

JAZZ

After the dissemination of jazz, which was definitely "put through" by the Dark Forces, a very marked decline in sexual morals became noticeable. Whereas at one time women were content with decorous flirtations, a vast number of them are now constantly preoccupied with the search for erotic adventures, and have thus turned sexual passion into a species of hobby. Now, it is just this overemphasis of the sex nature, this wrong attitude towards it, for which jazz music has been responsible. The orgiastic element about its syncopated rhythm, entirely divorced from any more exalted musical content, produced a hyper-excitement of the nerves and loosened the powers of self-control. It gave rise to a false exhilaration, a fictitious endurance, an insatiability resulting in a deleterious *moral* and physical reaction. Whereas the old-fashioned melodious dance music inspired the gentler sentiments, jazz, with its array of harsh, ear-splitting percussion-instruments, inflamed, intoxicated, and brutalised, thus causing a set-back in Man's nature towards the instincts of his racial childhood. For jazz music at its height very closely resembled the music of primitive savages. A further result of it was to be seen in the love of sensationalism which that has so greatly increased. As Jazz itself was markedly sensational, the public has increasingly come to demand "thrills" in the form of movies and plays, the only dramatic interest of which is connected with crime, mystery, and brutality. This also applies to sensational fiction: for the output and sale of this type is prodigious. The widespread and exaggerated interest taken in prize-fights is another symptom of sensationalism.

The latest cumulative effect of jazz is rock and roll, and those hysterical and unruly hero-worshipping exhibitions on the part of female teenagers aroused by the good looks and performances of some male crooner. Further, matters of sex are so bruited abroad that one can open hardly a single paper without being confronted with photos of almost naked women. In addition, the vulgar elements in jazz combined with its other ones have had such vulgarising effects, that we now have the misfortune to live in a vulgar and blatant age.

It should not be inferred from the above that the Masters regard sex per se as inherently evil: it is sexual excesses and sexual selfishness that are evil. And these are what jazz has tended to create; I say tended, because fortunately it does not operate on everyone.

In this connection, so as to avoid misunderstandings, it might be well to mention that one of the Masters, voicing the Hierarchy, has pointed out that the whole attitude towards sex during the Christian era has been a wrong one, for which St. Paul was responsible. When the Christ originated the Christian religion it was never His intention that such a disastrous attitude toward a natural function should obtain: disastrous, since it has been responsible for thousands of wrecked homes, divorces, suicides, murders, duels, and terrible suffering. And what has been the eventual outcome? Instead of a revolt against the unreasonable, intolerant, and uncharitable attitude itself, a large section of the young community has revolted against the idea of almost any form of sexual restraint. The part that a modernised form of primitive music has played in this revolt has already been implied.

The question may be asked: "Then why did the Higher Powers permit jazz to 'come through?'" And although to give an adequate answer would be to embark on a discussion as lengthy as the one involved by the momentous question: "Why does God allow evil?" Yet a few hints may be put forward.

If we can only perceive the isolated parts of a great spiritual Scheme, those parts in themselves may appear evil, but in conjunction with the whole they are really good. It was necessary for the spiritual progress of the race that both men and women should acquire a judicious measure of control, for its own sake, and *not* in view of any other considerations. In the Victorian era, women, being enclosed, so to speak, in the cages of convention, were not free to choose whether they would exercise control or not: they were *compelled* to suppress their passions, or invite consequences they dared not face. In the present century, however, conditions are so much changed that young people can find opportunities for sex gratification—if they so wish—with very little danger of detection. Thus, they have the choice whether they will learn the lesson of control or not, which brings us to answer the question why the Higher Powers permitted the diffusion of Jazz. It is because jazz music has tended to make that lesson rather more difficult, and consequently, the learning of it all the more conducive to spiritual evolution.

25

Musicians and Their Subtler Bodies

That the psychological organism of the artist, be he creator or interpreter, differs from that of the average man, most people are superficially prepared to admit. Wherein that difference lies, we propose in the light of occultism to examine. In the first place, the generality of artists function in the sympathetic system as opposed to the cerebral-spinal—that is to say—in the emotions rather than in the mind. This in itself constitutes one of their major difficulties for musicians in particular—whether creative or interpretative—frequently find themselves at the mercy of those very emotions they are endeavouring to sway in others. Being, so to say, recognised exponents of the emotions, and constantly meeting others who view them in that light, their personalities become subjected to emotional vortices, which few of them are capable of understanding or controlling, since they lack the power consciously to resist the turbulent thought-forms directed at them. Such power of resistance, indeed, can only be acquired when a measure of control over their own lower vehicles has been attained, and this is in itself not easy, for the average successful musical executant is endowed with a *positive* astral body as opposed to the *negative* one of the average man; hence, those disturbances that so often assail his passional nature.

The exact science of Sound being as yet unknown in the West, com-

140

posers and executants alike are not always able to discriminate among the innumerable influences to which their subtler vehicles are open. The composer in particular finds himself upon an uncharted sea while awaiting inspiration. What he receives and transmits may uplift and inspire, or it may do the reverse. His responsibility is great, yet for the most part he is unaware of the fact. There has always been a certain stream of inspiration emanating from the White Lodge, but whether it is, or has been, successfully contacted by any given composer or not, depends and has depended upon the state of his own inner development.

The difficulties of musicians have been further complicated by the influence of Devas playing through them, as was clearly demonstrated both in the case of Wagner and of Scriabin.

To adjust the inevitable discrepancy arising from the overshadowing of humans by entities who, as has been said, for the most part are unfamiliar with the limitations and exigencies of earth-life, the Masters have developed certain currents by which the relationship may be better coordinated. It remains to be seen how the artist of the future will react to the great opportunities thus afforded. Hitherto, the contacts have been sporadic and hence largely unsatisfactory; either the Devas have failed to influence the artist in a sufficiently rhythmic manner, or he has been unable to sustain the high vibration necessary for complete success. Now, however, certain Masters are specialising in the work of directing the *higher* types of Devas, suggesting to them what lines to adopt and deprecating those that have hitherto proved unfortunate and even disastrous in their results. But until the artist himself has learnt to discriminate *in his higher bodies* between the loftier type of Devas and the irresponsible element characteristic of the less evolved nature-spirits, it were wiser for him to postpone all conscious attempts to co-operate with these entities until a future incarnation. Such co-operation, it should be added, will necessitate an intense stimulation of the *causal body,* which, only by degrees, will make itself perceptible to the physical brain-consciousness. In this way only the higher Devas reporting to the Masters will be contacted, and all influences of a less desirable nature excluded. This will be the sole recognised line, which will have the co-operation of the Lodge, as it was found that an earlier method, which consisted in arousing the physical centres to a state of awareness to nature-spirits *first,* proved exceedingly dangerous if adopted by irresponsible or unscrupulous people.

All those, both in and out of incarnation, who can safely contact the Devas are known to the Lodge by the particular note they sound out on the inner planes. These are tested and learn to work with them while out of their physical bodies, long before they realise what is being attempted on this plane. Only if the Master thinks fit do they bring through into waking consciousness the knowledge of how to invoke the Devas, and then solely for the helping of their fellow men; without such a safeguard, and should this knowledge become general, those bent on the acquisition of personal power would be able to compel the Devas to do their will, thus repeating the terrible errors of Atlantis.

In order to further this new relationship between Devas and artists, the music of the near future will tend to become more harmonious than of recent years (see chapter 36) and inspired with the idea of helping Man to obtain greater poise in and control of his lower vehicles. Only when such poise and control have been to a very considerable measure attained will the Great Ones deem it safe or possible to allow the Buddhic music, in the fullness of its supernal beauty, to be given to the world. Were it "put through" prematurely, there is grave risk of undesirable reactions upon unbalanced temperaments.

To a certain extent the more mental music previously alluded to will resemble the Indian *mantra* (this subject will be considered in chapter 27), but with this difference, that whereas the ancient priest-musician strove to raise his consciousness to the mental plane in order to escape the menace of his emotional nature, the future exponent of sound, with mind fully controlled, will invoke the denizens of the higher planes to *descend* and inspire him. Everything that can be done to assist this development will have the blessing and guidance of the Lodge, for this process of the higher *descending* into the lower self constitutes one of the keys to the future evolution of the race for centuries to come.

PART IV
Historical
Melody and Harmony from Pre-Egyptian Times to Nineteenth-Century England

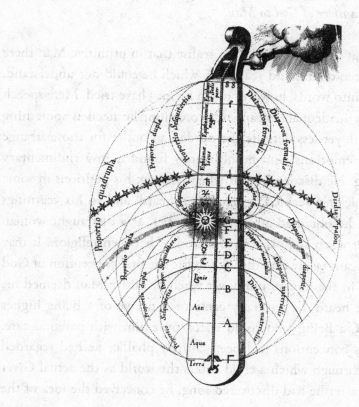

26

The Beginnings of Music and Religion

Whereas Melody is the cry of Man to God, Harmony is the answer of God to Man.

It requires but little imagination to realise that in primitive Man there must have been desires and yearnings, which he could not understand, still less put into words, however much he may have tried. Mere speech was a totally inadequate means of expression; he needed something more forceful, yet less definite; he needed an outlet for those strange supplicatory emotions: and he ultimately found it in a rudimentary form of song. He discovered that when he sang, his petitions in some unaccountable way seemed to have been heard, and so his yearnings were stilled; he obtained an emotional relief, as a distraught woman obtains relief when she prays to the God of her own religion. It may seem extravagant to say that through music the first conception of God was aroused in the human mind, yet when primitive Man deemed his prayers were heard, he naturally came to conceive of a Being higher than himself, a Being who could watch over him with parental care. Hitherto his conceptions had been entirely phallic; he had regarded "the portal through which a child enters the world as the actual Giver of life"; but after he had discovered song, he conceived the idea of the

Great Mother, the very first deity to whom he turned for consolation and protection from the evils of his precarious existence.[1]

The next stage in the evolution of religion is common knowledge; when once the idea of the Great Mother had been formulated, Man fashioned her image in wood or stone, and carved figures of her in caves, for he felt the need of a concrete object toward which to direct his worship. Finally, having fashioned his idols, he appointed someone to guard them and minister to their supposed needs; and in this manner the office of priest originated. It was the priests who by degrees improved the primitive type of song and transformed it into a species of chanted spell. These spells were committed to memory and handed down from generation to generation. Only much later were they notated. One of their effects was to increase religious fervour, with the result that men began to sway with their bodies, to dance, and clap their hands. In the course of time the most elementary form of drum was invented to accentuate the rhythm; this led to the invention of other instruments and so to the actual birth of music as an art.

We see, then, that from the very beginning, music was associated with religion, and that the priests played an important part in its systematisation and development. Indeed, according to the Akashic Records, the first priest who was selfless enough pure-heartedly to serve humanity was enabled to hear the music of the higher spheres; and to him it was given to know that whereas "Melody is the cry of Man to God, Harmony is the answer of God to Man." But although, needless to say, he was unable to translate what he heard into earthly sounds— the means being lacking—it inspired him with the idea of introducing a greater variety into the existing musical phrases, so from that time onward, music very gradually became more diversified.

The priests, having discovered the potency of the above mentioned *mantrams* or spells, and realising that if certain notes were reiterated definite results could be obtained and definite powers brought into action, used this particular form of magic—for magic it was—for noble and constructive ends during the earlier periods of Atlantean history. Under the influence of Initiates, Sound was employed to build beautiful and wonder inspiring forms; but in the later phases of that mighty civilisation it came to be employed entirely as a force for destruction. Discordant sounds were deliberately used to shatter and disintegrate. As every occultist knows, the practice of magic for evil ends was responsible for the downfall of the continent, and thus perished not only that dark phase of its music, but also that scientific knowledge of the application and potency of Sound that had wrought such havoc. Wherever some particular power or aspect of knowledge has become vitiated by abuse, it has been permitted by the Higher Ones to fall for the time being into obscurity, to re-emerge again aeons later, perhaps, as a purified overtone of itself.

Among the first composers to be instrumental in introducing this overtone of the ancient Atlantean music was Debussy. In more occult terms he was unconsciously used by the Higher Ones to carry over Fourth Race sound-vibrations into the Fifth. To this end he made a study of and absorbed the characteristics of Javanese music, which is a remnant, though mellowed and modified, of the Atlantean, and which, I should add, exercises a powerful influence through the astral on the physical body, especially on the solar plexus. An obvious example of this Fourth Race music mingling with that of the Fifth is shown in his *Fêtes* in which ancient chants actually associated with the temples of the past subtly mingle with a wholly modern and irresponsible element.

Debussy was succeeded by composers unconsciously expressing the harsher and more destructive elements of the Atlantean music, albeit at a higher point of the evolutionary spiral, since, as I elaborated in chapter 22, this destructive force is used to disintegrate obsolete and baneful thought-forms of various kinds.

We will now return to the consideration of music in another and earlier phase of its development.

27

Effects of Music on the Indian People

Wisdom is subtilised, spiritualised knowledge.

If we point out to an Indian that his music lacks variety, he will not understand us. Has he not gay music and solemn music and sad music, therefore, what more can be needed? Moreover, he will argue that he has four divisions to the tone, and we have only two. And, in answer, we will confront him with our enormous orchestras, our pianos, organs, and huge choruses: can his few mellow-toned instruments compare with such an array?

The characteristics of Indian music, then, are not those of volume but of subtlety, seeing that it has quarter-tones; and there are cogent reasons both for its qualities and its limitations. When the *Manu*, or Ruler, founded the Fifth Root Race in India, in order to counteract the Black Magic prevalent among the Fourth Root Race Atlanteans, from whom he was obliged to select his nucleus, he forbade the playing of the existent music, the effects of which had proved so disastrous, and inaugurated a new scale and science of *mantrams*, so that the new sub-race might respond to higher vibrations and learn to reach the mental plane. These *mantrams* were handed down by Indian priests through the centuries that followed, became entirely associated with religious traditions, and were only to be performed at set times of the day. Thus, there would be the chant to be sung before the early meditation, the chant for noon, the chant for sunset, each calculated to have a specific effect upon singer and audience alike. And after all these ages, so powerful is the influence of religious tradition in India, that no one would think to perform, say, the early-morning chant at noon, still less at sunset.

The ancient Indian priests, then, instead of seeking to develop music as an art, sought merely to enhance its *mantramistic* value. They were already contemplative by nature, and having realised that certain sequences of notes produced profound meditation, they experimented with them and subtilised them until they achieved the desired result; that result was *Samadhi,* or superconscious trance. But although in that state of trance they heard the "music of vision"—if the term may be pardoned—they made no effort to translate it into earthly sound; they were content that it should remain simply a means of attaining union with the Divine through its power to assist meditation. When man has reached Bliss, what else is there for him to attain or desire? Like the Psalmist, these ancient Indian priests considered that "the fear of the Lord is the beginning of Wisdom, and the knowledge of the Holy One is understanding." The result was the evolving of those exalted systems of religious philosophy, which have ever remained as a monument to the greatness of Indian thought. Because the quarter-tone itself was so subtle, it subtilized the mind, in addition to inducing contemplative trance, and the outcome was not merely the acquisition of knowledge, but of Wisdom, for Wisdom is but *subtilised, spiritualised* knowledge.

Nevertheless, it would be incorrect to say that Indian music remained entirely *mantramistic* and trance-inducing; there were yearnings and aspirations in the people themselves, which must find a vent in melody; there were also purely human passions that evoked suffering and impelled the unphilosophically-minded to pour themselves out in song. But even so, as no instruments capable of expressing fervour, energy, or power had been invented, the means at their disposal were limited; hence, Indian music has remained largely of the homophonic, restricted type. An art so circumscribed, into which comes no novelty of idea, which, in short, does not progress, is apt to fade into insignificance. If music in the West had remained stationary, it too, would have suffered a similar fate.

That Indian music affected chiefly the mind, we have endeavoured to show; furthermore, because it lacked in general those more energising elements of our varied Western music, we find that the people of India lack those elements also. Climate may, of course, be to some extent responsible for this, but a vitalising type of music could have largely modified its influence. Inasmuch as their music lacked variety, lacked energy, lacked power, so have the Indians themselves as a race remained one-sided, inert, and unequally balanced in character. Apart from the warrior caste there are few men of action; the bulk of the people are dreamy, meditative, and given over in excess to the things of the spirit.

Yet the question will be asked: is one really justified in attributing the characteristics of a whole nation to *music*? Is that not carrying the assumption too far? Yes, but only if we fail to take into account its indirect as well as its direct influence.

When we come away from a concert at which the last item on the programme has been something grand and majestic, do we not feel inspired with the longing to perform great and heroic actions? Or, if that is not consistent with our temperament, do we not at least feel within us an added power and vitality? Have we not been stirred in a manner in which hardly any other medium of expression *but* music can stir us? It is true the effect wears off after a while, but the experience is repeated the next time we hear music of a similar kind. And suppose that we are constantly hearing music, day after day, week after week, year after year, will those constantly repeated emotions leave no imprint upon our character, our emotional nature? Then there is the influence of heredity to consider. As the love of music itself is often transmitted from parent to child or grandchild, is it not probable that the effects of that music upon character will also be transmitted? And if that music, as in India, has been passed on through scores of generations, will its effects not have become correspondingly intensified? If we admit this, we shall understand the characteristic lethargy of the Indian people. We shall also realize that if they *are* one-sided, they are mainly suffering from the defects of their qualities, and that only the contemplative temperament of their forebears could have bequeathed to the world such incomparable systems of philosophy.

28

The Music and Character of the Ancient Egyptians

*Every faith has its appropriate music, and the difference
between the creeds might almost be expressed in musical
notation.*

Sir James George Frazer, *The Golden Bough*

Religion is a cult of certain of the emotions.

Fielding Hall, *The Hearts of Men*

We now come to deal with the effect of music on the Egyptians, and
the part it played in their mighty civilisation. For if we have treated
Indian music first in order, it is not because it was the most ancient,
but because it was the most subtle: our intention being to proceed from
subtle to gross; from the quarter-tone to the third-tone, and finally to
the half-tone.

It was the third-tone that characterised the music of Egypt, and so
rendered it one degree less subtle than that of India, with the result that

instead of working upon the mind, it stopped short at the emotions, because the emotional organism is itself less subtle than the mentality. As for example, the vibrations produced by the ultra-violet rays are too subtle to affect the organs of human vision, so are the vibrations produced by the quarter-tone too subtle to affect, at any rate directly, the human emotional make-up.

Now, as we have already said, when the mind is subtilised, spiritualized, it becomes the instrument of Wisdom. But this is not so when left to function in the normal way, for then it is solely the instrument of knowledge, though only when unhampered and undisturbed by the coarser emotions. Indeed, the latter, if excited and out of control, are hostile to knowledge, for they tarnish, so to say, the reflector of the mind; on the other hand, when they are calm and controlled, they leave the reasoning faculties in full possession, and the result is common sense and lucidity of thought.

And it was just this result, which the Egyptians achieved with their third-tone, tended to calm the emotional organism and to purge it of its grosser vibrations. But what is more, it tended in certain circumstances to induce an emotional species of trance.

An examination of ancient religion reveals the fact that schools for the study of Esotericism existed (and still exist) in every civilisation worthy of the name: schools in which the pupil was taught not only to believe in the finer elements of Nature, but actually to know them. In Egypt these esoteric schools were called "The Mysteries," and in one of their most important ceremonies of initiation, the candidate, with the aid of music and other rites, was precipitated into a trance, from which he emerged with knowledge of the post-mortem states of existence. For the third-tone under certain conditions tended to loosen the emotional body from the physical and so induce an "astral trance." Through this latter he learned from actual experience that he was immortal: he had not only visited the higher planes, but also the lowest and most horrible; he had descended into "hell," risen again, and ascended into "heaven," as the Christian creed phrases it: for the latter is but an adaptation of the Egyptian rubric. We must, however, not confound the trance of the

Egyptian with that of the Indian sage: the latter was concerned with experiencing spiritual Bliss, the former with acquiring occult knowledge; the one was a mystic, the other more of a scientist. And not only was he concerned with the gaining of knowledge, but with devising the necessary means to gain it: in a word, he was a magician. Just as the scientist experiments in order to establish the right conditions for the discovery of some scientific fact, so also does the magician: the only difference is that the scientist works with Nature's grosser forces, the magician with her finer ones. It is, indeed, to the Egyptian civilisation that we of the West owe all ceremonial magic: the Christian Mass originated in Egypt, and not in Jerusalem, even though it is said to have been introduced in the Church to commemorate the Last Supper.

Before we pass from the subject of Esotericism and Magic, two significant facts should be mentioned. Firstly, the Egyptians regarded music itself as having a divine origin; secondly, they held that harmony and the various instruments had been discovered and invented by the gods. Thus, according to them, Hermes discovered the principle of concerted voices and sounds, and was the inventor of the lyre and the earliest form of guitar, while to Osiris was attributed the invention of the flute. Nor are these suppositions at variance with the esoteric side of the Egyptian religion: for at one time the so-called gods were men— great Adepts, great King-Initiates—who walked the earth and ruled the people. And just because they were so great they were deified, as the Founder of Christianity has been deified and His disciples canonised. And yet just as—esoterically considered—the masses of today may be said to be ignorant of the truth respecting *their* Teacher, so were the masses in Egypt ignorant of the truth respecting their gods.

Even the priests were not admitted indiscriminately to the honour of initiation . . . the Egyptians neither entrusted the knowledge of the "Mysteries" to everyone, nor degraded the secrets of divine matters by disclosing them to the profane: they reserved them for the heir apparent to the throne, and for *such priests* as excelled in virtue and wisdom.[1]

It will be seen, then, that the conception of the gods of Egypt was *not* merely the outcome of base and ignorant superstitions, but the logical result of knowledge gained through initiation. That in the course of time that knowledge became corrupted and diffused itself, so to say, into superstition, is true, but it did not thus originate. The Egyptian religion in its pure and pristine state was as exalted and philosophical as the Vedic religion; its fundamental doctrine being the Unity of God, and Jesus adopted a similar policy, entrusting disciples with teachings He did not give to the populace that from God emanated Man, and to Him he would ultimately return.* Thus, the Egyptian believed in the immortality of the soul, and consequently he also believed that those "Great Ones" whom he or his ancestors had loved and revered, still lived on, even though they had passed into higher spheres. It was no more illogical for him to offer them his tributes or pray to them than for the Roman Catholic to pray to his patron saint: for as the modern spiritualist believes that the spirits of the departed can in certain circumstances guard and console him, so did the ancient Egyptian. But this did not preclude him from accepting the basic doctrine of one God, any more than the fact of a multitude of individuals precludes the Vedic idea of the One Consciousness, the One Self. Nor did it prevent him from dividing God into His attributes when He would be called the Creator, the Divine Goodness, Wisdom, Power, and so forth. It is true that in order to convey an impression of these abstract ideas to the eye it was deemed necessary to distinguish them by some fixed representation, hence gods and goddesses multiplied to an extraordinary extent. Yet these figures were never intended to be looked upon as real personages: they were symbols and nothing more.

We need not dwell any longer on the religion of Egypt; we have attempted to show that it was the outcome of logical, philosophical investigation and thought—of a penetration into Nature's subtler forces, in brief, of Occultism in its higher forms. Unfortunately, how-

---

*As Wordsworth has phrased it:
  Trailing clouds of Glory do we come
  From God who is our home.

ever, certain superstitions arose to tarnish its purity; selfishness crept into its occultism, and the merely relative occult truths were substituted for absolute ones.

It was known that the gross physical body exercised a very mysterious but strong attraction over the departed ego, and that as long as the former remained intact, the link between the two was not severed. Because the Indians recognized this, they burned their dead, so that the "spirit" might be liberated at once. But selfishness impelled the Egyptians to do exactly the reverse; they sought to preserve the body in order that the spirit might remain in touch with the earth, and consequently *with themselves.* How the idea of mummification first arose— whether to preserve that which had been held in so much honour or for other reasons we will not here discuss—but, as finally practised, it was a perversion of occult knowledge to personal ends. Indeed, knowledge when divorced from Wisdom and the sense of Unity almost invariably results in selfishness: and through selfishness came the downfall of the Egyptian civilisation.

It remains to be seen why this was the case, and in what way music was connected with that downfall.

Although music plays a great part in our European life, it played an even greater one in that of Egypt; there seemed to be hardly an activity of the daily round with which it was not associated. Whatever their occupations might be, the Egyptians always worked to the strains of a song; they sang when they sowed, they sang when they harvested, the women sang as they wove, and the hosts of men sang as they transported a colossus from the great stone quarries. And their singing was not of the sporadic type, which characterises that of the European labourer, it was organised and especially suited to the particular occupation in which they were engaged. There was even somebody to beat time by clapping his hands: for the Egyptians realised that concerted singing facilitated labour, just as martial music encouraged the soldier when he set forth to war . . . That music played an important role in all ritual, at all festivities, banquets, receptions, funerals, and religious festivities, we need hardly mention; what *is* noteworthy is that it was of a far more varied character than the music of India with which we have already dealt. If we consider that there were lyres, guitars, harps of various sizes, flutes, pipes and double pipes, trumpets, cymbals, and drums, we realise that a fair volume as well as variety of sound must have been produced. And this being so, there were types of music to calm the emotions and conversely to stir them. Thus, the temperament of the Egyptian was, unlike that of the Indian, a balanced one. Owing to the generally sooth-ing effect of the third-tone on his emotional nature, he was neither con-stantly "in a whirl," nor yet lethargic and devoid of initiative; he struck, or rather endeavoured to strike the fair medium, just as his music, taken as a whole, struck that fair medium. It even contained to a certain small extent the divine quality of harmony; and we read—significantly—that the lyre was deemed especially suited to religious ceremonies, because on the lyre could be played *chords*.

All the same—for we now come to a critical question—if Egyptian music exercised such a beneficial, such a well-rounded effect on char-acter, how came it that selfishness and superstition brought about the downfall of the Egyptian civilisation? Was its music, notwithstanding its good qualities, directly or indirectly responsible? And the answer is a noteworthy one: it was not owing to what Egyptian music possessed, but to what it *lacked,* that Egypt fell. As India had ultimately fallen because it had spiritual Wisdom but not concrete knowledge, so con-versely Egypt fell because it had concrete knowledge but not spiritual wisdom. For knowledge gives power, and power all too often engenders *love* of power; then comes the final step, love of *personal* power—in a word—selfishness with its inevitable consequence: disintegration of the community. When each individual is trying to gain the ascendency over his neighbour, instead of to co-operate with him, how, indeed, can it be other wise? There is nothing in the universe that can remain for long intact when forces of whatsoever nature are all pulling in different directions. In a word, since Egyptian music was entirely lacking in the wisdom-inspiring aspect, and as its harmonic or divine aspect was too limited to be strongly operative, Egypt went to its doom, as did Greece and Rome after it. As in 1914 and 1939, the nations of Europe, because they likewise lacked wisdom, prostituted their scientific knowledge and used it for diabolical purposes, so did the Egyptian prostitute his occult knowledge. Moreover, coincident with his ethical decline, his music began to deteriorate, and the small amount of harmony disappeared. Instead of being developed, it was gradually forgotten; musical taste became lower and lower, and although the third-tone remained, it was used for trivial purposes, just as our own half-tone may be, and often *is* so used. Thus what might have grown to be the finest music dwindled into utter insignificance.

We have stated the prime cause: let us now examine the secondary causes.

The evil began with the priesthood. As already said, many of the priests had at one time been initiated into the Mysteries, but in the course of years fewer and fewer were found to be worthy of that honour: they were deficient in the essential qualities. Instead of manifesting self-lessness, instead of working disinterestedly for humanity, they showed signs of egoism and a liking for power. And, of course, as this increased it eventually became an intense love of power; the love of beauty, truth, and the higher emotions decreased in proportion, together with their love of music, that medium through which those higher emotions were expressed. They grew indifferent and careless of how the sacred music was rendered, and eventually of what standard of music was employed. Thus, as the exalted influence of the sacred music was withdrawn, the character, not only of the priests but of the people, gradually degener-ated. With the little knowledge which that had filtered through from the lesser Mysteries, much of the true significance of which had been forgotten, the priests worked on the minds of the populace "and para-lyzed their reasoning powers; the result being that the Egyptians gave way to the grossest superstitions, which at length excited universal ridi-cule and contempt."[2] But, unfortunately, what the historian was content to term "superstition" was in reality of a far more harmful nature: it was the subjugation of occult forces for evil ends; and when a nation resorts to this its doom is inevitable.

29

The Greeks and Their Music

With Greece we come to the half-tone and to European music. As the quarter-tone of India worked especially on the mental, and the third-tone of Egypt especially on the emotional, the half-tone of Greece worked especially on the material or physical. Thus, we have passed from subtle to less subtle, and finally to gross: below this, music can no longer be termed music but mere sound or noise.

It must not be assumed that there was no music of any kind in Europe prior to Greece; music existed to a certain extent in other countries, where it had originated in supplication to the Deity, and had been employed by the priesthood; but Greece was the first European country to bring it to a state of comparative perfection: it became an art, and in one sense even a science. Cicero states that the Greeks

> considered the arts of singing and playing upon musical instruments
> a very principal part of learning. . . . Hence Greece became cele-
> brated for skilful musicians; and, as all persons there studied music,
> those who attained to no proficiency in it were thought uneducated
> and unaccomplished.

Nor was the latter reflection a surprising one, seeing the great philosophers and poets had extolled music, and that it was supposed to be of divine origin and presided over by Apollo, the ever young and beautiful god.

Although many phases of Egyptian music were carried over into Greece, Grecian music cannot be said to have actually originated in Egypt. More correct were is it to say that in the course of time the Greeks adopted a large number of Egyptian instruments and elaborated or adjusted them to their modal needs. The flute, for instance, originally Egyptian, had at first only four holes, but later "Diodorus of Thebes in Boeotia added others, and made a lateral opening for the mouth. It was originally of reed, afterwards of bone or ivory." Of other reed instruments there were the single and double pipes, both being quite common in Greece and Egypt, also the syrinx. As for stringed instruments there was a variety of lyres, harps, and cithars (a type of guitar). Of percussion there was also a fair variety; and it is to Greece that we owe our tambourine with its metal attachments, though the simpler type hailed from Egypt. We need hardly point out that with so much instrumental material, harmony—though of a limited kind—formed a part of Greek music; and to this, combined with the effects of the half-tone, we attribute that admixture of religion and superstition so peculiar to the Greek people.

Having described the instruments of Greece, a few words should be added relative to the Greek scales or *modes,* as they are termed. Of these, the ancient Greeks possessed originally but three, the Dorian, the Phrygian, and the Lydian, but subsequently they were increased to seven. If—to explain these modes—our modern scale of C, which is all on white keys, be played from E to E, the disposition of tones and semi-tones is that of the Dorian; if from D to D, that of the Phrygian.* And it is significant that various emotional and ethical effects were attributed by the eminent Greek thinkers to melodies founded on these various modes. The Dorian was said to inspire courage, self-esteem,

---

*The others are the Hypolydian, F to F; the Hypophrygian, G to G; the Hypodorian, A to A; the Mixoludian, B to B.

and respect for the law; the Lydian to induce voluptuous feelings; and the Phrygian repose, dignity and self-control. But unfortunately those thinkers—who included Plato and Aristotle—were not all of the same opinion regarding these scales and their effects, the reason being that they overlooked several important factors: the instruments employed, the *tempi,* and so forth. For instance, taking our full list of orchestral instruments and dividing them into four categories, it is, broadly speaking, correct to say that (1) drums and brass affect the physical, (2) reeds the emotional, (3) strings the mental-emotional, (4) harp and organ the spiritual-emotional. Nevertheless, if a certain type of music be played, say, on the brass, and, as naturally follows, played in a certain way, or in conjunction with other instruments taking a subordinate part, the effect may be quite the opposite of a physical one. The same applies to both the reeds and strings, and even to the percussion. Who has not experienced the purely emotional influence of muffled drums, or that of a cymbal struck *pianissimo* with a drumstick? However, when either of these instruments is used in a more vigorous manner it operates entirely on the physical.

And so when the great men of Hellas ascribed different influences to the various modes, their assertions were not of necessity incorrect, though on the surface they appeared contradictory. Indeed, in connection with many of our own assertions relative to the half-tone and its influence on the physical, we may, like those ancient philosophers, appear to contradict ourselves. It should, therefore, be clearly understood that when we maintain that the semi-tone works directly on the physical, we do not for a moment imply that it has no *indirect* effect on the emotions or the mind. To say that some passage played from *Parsifal,* for example, operates exclusively upon the physical body, were, of course, absurd. The essential truth for the reader to grasp is that as a general tendency the half-tone affects the physical plane, or, perhaps better expressed, man's attitude to the physical plane. As the conquest of Spirit was the most pronounced feature of the great day of ancient Indian civilisation, the conquest of Matter has been the most pronounced feature of European civilisation. And this, we contend, is due to the general and increasing effects of the half-tone. When, however, a variety of other factors came by slow degrees to be connected with this our Western division of the scale, Man came to occupy himself once more with "the things of the spirit," but from a different standpoint and motive from those of his Aryan forefathers. But we shall have some way to travel before we reach the musical effects, which are associated with this momentous impulse to "return to God," as the mystics have phrased it. For the present, we are concerned with the effects of the half-tone at the time of its inception.

One need only look at the plastic arts of Greece to realise what an important part the *physical* played in Grecian civilisation. It is obvious that the one aim of the painter or the sculptor was to depict physical perfection; it is also obvious that all Greek art was uncoloured by the emotions: it was entirely "thought out," a product of the unemotionalized mind. If, for instance, we compare Egyptian paintings with those of Greece, we find, as we do with many modern paintings, that they are untrue to nature: or, phrased otherwise, they depict nature as seen through the emotions. But of Greek sculpture and painting the very reverse must be said: they were not only true to nature, but, if the paradox be allowed, they were even truer than nature. It was for this reason that Aristotle was impelled to remark: "Even if it is impossible that men should be such as Zeuxis painted them, yet it is better he should paint them so; for the example ought to excel that for which it is an example." This very word, in fact, gives us the clue to the whole theory of Greek art, namely, the blending of the beautiful and the good: the aesthetic and the ethical.

And how highly significant this educative conception of art—for educative it was—in view of what we have written regarding Greek music! Ethics deal with the regulation of conduct, and conduct is associated with action—that is to say—the physical. When the mind is not disturbed by undesirable emotions, man acts rightly; for, as we hardly need hardly point out, right thought is the director of right action. Thus, the science of ethics as understood in Greece was neither the product of subtilised thought nor of emotional religious thought, but

of pure reasoning in connection with the sphere of action—in a word—
the physical. Moreover, as we progress with the study of Greek life, we
shall see how nearly every phase of it either started from or was brought
down to the physical.

To pass on from art to the exoteric side of religion with which it
was so closely interwoven—the religion as understood not by Initiates
like Plato and Pythagoras—but by the people. Expressed concisely, this
religion was the reduction of the forces of Nature to concrete personalities; it was even more: it was the reduction of human passions to concrete personalities. In order to explain natural phenomena, the ancient
Greek posited beings of spirits resembling himself, but mightier than
himself; to explain emotional phenomena he did likewise. When he saw
the storm approaching across the darkened sea, he saw with his mind's
eye spirits who caused the anger of wind and waves; and when he felt a
storm within himself and the angry billows of passion beating against
his heart, he saw their cause as external to himself: he had permitted the
spirits of evil to obsess him. In this way originated the idea of a host of
gods and goddesses, of sprites and nymphs, of nereids and dryads. But
be it noted, those beings had a form, however ethereal, similar to that
of man himself, and as a proof of this we possess the legacy of Grecian
art. The statues of the gods were simply representations of the highest
physical perfection; they were not symbolic as were the images of India.
Where in Greece can be found such an embodied idea as Shiva, the
Destroyer? Although the Greek gods were by no means morally perfect,
not one sculptor thought to portray them other than beautiful; a Greek
Shiva would have been regarded in the light of blasphemy.

And now what may be said of the relation of man to the gods?
As Mr. Lowes Dickenson points out, it was a purely mechanical one;[1]
neither mystical nor spiritual. It was a relation pertaining to the physical plane, and bearing the nature of a contract or bargain. Conscience,
as the Christian understands that word, did not exist for the ancient
Greek. If he had offended the gods, all he was sensible of was fear; he
deemed they would punish him for his offence. The form that punishment would take might be sickness or misfortune: in any case it would

be connected with this physical life. Merely to be forgiven by the gods for the asking was not to be thought of; he must offer them gifts, sacrifice to them, flatter them—there was no other way—were they not beings, with vanities and passions like himself?

Yet despite this material conception, the Greeks believed in a future life, but they were even less anxious to experience it than is the average Christian. They were far too happy with the joys of the physical world to wish for those of the superphysical; indeed, many of their great poets and dramatists painted the whole after-death state in colours of the utmost pessimism. Instead of welcoming death, they regarded it and its forerunner old age with something approaching horror; to grow old and be no longer physically attractive was for them the saddest of prospects. How widely different from the attitude of the Hindu, so engrossed in thoughts of "heaven" as almost entirely to neglect the things of earth!

As the Hindu was all for dreamy contemplation, the Greek was all for action, athletic excitement, games, contests, heroic deeds; in fine, the glorification of the physical. Even into friendships between members of the same sex the physical entered, not because the Greeks were an utterly depraved and licentious people—far from it—but rather because it was the inevitable outcome of their entire conception of life. They saw in the physical body the most beautiful of the gods' creations, and worshipped it accordingly. And the law was with them in this; passionate friendships between men, instead of being prohibited, were actually an institution. With the Greeks passion was not so much a matter of sex as of love, and hence it was a purer type of passion than that of other nations, although on the surface it may have seemed less so. Thus legislators, instead of regarding homosexuality as hostile to law and order, encouraged it; to them it was not something impure, but even advantageous to the State. As such passionate friendships were usually between an older and a younger man, the former exercised a beneficial influence upon the latter's mind: he educated and developed him.[2] To many of us nowadays, of course, sexual irregularities, even when coupled with idealism, seem repugnant, but that is merely because our point of view is so radically different from that of the ancient Greeks. Puritanism has left its sombre hues upon our morals: puritanism, that strange attitude of mind, which regards nearly everything beautiful as anti-spiritual, though changes are now perceptible. But to the Greek nature it was utterly foreign, as was hypocrisy, that other attribute with which it is so closely allied. So little did the Greeks understand of either of these, that Demosthenes in open court declared that every married man "requires at least two mistresses."[3] Such *liaisons*, in fact, were not only approved by custom, but were actually consistent with religion.

Were there not temples in honour of Aphrodite Pandemos, the goddess of illicit love?

It will be seen then that the physical element played a prodigious part in every phase of Greek life; and we will now briefly turn our attention, first to the esoteric side of Hellenistic thought; and, second, to the various schools of philosophy that flourished around the fifth and fourth centuries before Christ.

As every student knows, the Mysteries existed in Greece as they existed in Egypt, where they originated; there were also strange cults such as the cult of Dionysus, the god of inspiration and wine. Yet although the Mysteries have come to possess a historical fame, they did not form an integral part of popular religious thought. We must not make the mistake of confounding the ideas set forth by some of the famous Greek writers—who were initiated into the Mysteries—with the ideas of the ordinary people. Great thinkers, be they reformers, poets, or philosophers, are not a product of national thought, but vice versa; national thought is, or may be, the product of great thinkers; these set the ideal, and in the course of time the people live up to that ideal or not, according to circumstances.

And so, in reviewing the effects of Greek music on the thought, character, and life of the Greeks, we do not include Plato, Pythagoras, and several other eminent writers. It is, in fact, well known that far from endorsing Greek polytheistic ideas, Plato was fundamentally a monotheist; and as to the famous dramatists, some of them permitted themselves much sarcastic gaiety in connection with the current religious beliefs. Thus, the mysticism to be found in the works of Greek philosophers was not representative of Grecian thought, and the mysticism to be found associated with the cult of Dionysus, for instance, was but another example of the physical as basis, for its rites show that although their aim was to induce a "mystical" state of consciousness, the means employed were of a physical nature. In striking contrast to the Indian Yogi, who, using the mind only, sits with closed eyes motionless in a cave, every means was employed to stimulate the *senses*. Music in which percussion instruments predominated and worked directly on the nerves, "dances convulsing every limb and dazzling the eyes and brain, inebriating drinks, these formed a part of those strange revels described by Euripides in the 'Bacchae.'"[4] They were, in fact, merely a form of Dervish dance or Salvation Army meeting, both of which achieve certain emotional effects through an over-excitation of the physical nerves.

And now to mention the schools of philosophy for which Greece has come to be so renowned. The Platonic and Pythagorean were the outcome of Initiation, and, as the music used in the Mysteries was of a specific order not given forth to the people, the popular music of Greece cannot be said to have influenced those esoteric schools. With regard to the others, they were, like Greek art, the product of unemotionalised mind; they were simply formed, to use the colloquial phrase, by "thinking things out." Critical persons came to find that the gods and their behaviour did not bear the test of scrutiny, so there arose a spirit similar to that which in the middle of last century was termed agnosticism. True it is that materialistic philosophers who denied the gods had existed in Greece all along, in other words, a certain conflict between religion and science did not come suddenly into being; but it was only by the fifth century BC that it assumed such formidable proportions and became so pronounced that the general belief in the gods was seriously undermined. Nor was this all; eventually philosophers arose who even undermined the foundations of politics and ethics, in fine, scepticism was rife; and had not Plato appeared to adjust the balance by revealing a judicious portion of esoteric teaching, materialism would have spread far and wide.

It will no doubt read strangely if we say that the self-same agent, which produced religion, produced its antithesis—atheism—yet owing to the peculiar nature of the Greek religion, such was the case. As we have already stated, and others before us, the religion of Greece with all its supernaturalism was but a glorified *materialistic belief.* The gods, to summarise, were but grandiose human beings with all the passions of the latter, and the relationship between man and these gods was little better than that between man and man. Herein lies the explanation why the music, which tended to produce the Greek religion, tended also to produce scepticism and materialism. For it must especially be noted in connection with music (and this book) that the same cause does not invariably produce the same effects; if this were the case, it would only be necessary to play a hymn in order to make people religious; what it *does* produce is a fundamental *similarity* of effect, or, more simply put, effects which are akin but not absolutely alike. Now, there is no *fundamental* difference between the believer and the sceptic; the former is incredulous about one set of theories or facts, the latter is incredulous about another set: That is all. The believer cannot believe that the whole universe is fashioned by Chance, and the sceptic cannot believe that it is fashioned by God or the gods. To the believer the sceptic's attitude seems unreasonable and absurd, and to the sceptic the believer's attitude seems equally unreasonable and absurd. The Greek atheist might have argued with his opponent: "I believe in the all-sufficiency of matter itself—I require to posit no unseen but materialistic gods. . . ." Yet the whole contention turned on the question of matter, when all is said; each party was materialistic in its own manner.

We have shown how the mighty civilisation of Egypt declined; and it now remains to show the underlying cause why Greece followed so disastrously in its wake.

The Egyptians fell through love of power, the Greeks through love of beauty "run riot." As time progressed, they became more and more voluptuous and preoccupied with the pleasures of the senses, thus withdrawing their energy from the mind and its activities; in consequence, they lost their powers of perception and of reasoning. As with the Egyptians—for these comparisons are instructive—their downfall came about through a perversion of their chief characteristic. The third-tone of Egyptian music had been a strong factor in producing occult science, and through a perversion of that science its civilisation declined; similarly, the half-tone of Greek music had been a strong factor in producing the cult of physical beauty, with the same disastrous result. Nor does the similarity end here: both with Egyptian and Greek music, not only was the wisdom-engendering quarter-tone lacking, but the harmonic or religio-devotional aspect was insufficient to adjust the balance. Had it been more pronounced, it would have diverted much of the Greek love of physical beauty into higher channels; into love of *spiritual* beauty; but for this it was too meagre, too crude. Moreover, the little there was died out, and so harmony vanished from Greek music as it had done from Egyptian music.

Other changes also took place; the more sensuous strains of the viol were finally substituted for those of stronger-toned instruments, and musical taste altogether became weak and effeminate; merely a means of titillating the senses. In place of true artists, a great increase in the number of mere *virtuosi* had occurred, and the predominant influence of these in music must nearly always be looked upon as the first step in its downward course. For instance, in the year 456 BCE, Phrynis, the Citharoede, aroused great enthusiasm by his wonderful execution of scale passages. . . . Moreover, the same striving after effect, observable among the performers on the flute and lyre, had also begun to show itself among the singers. Instead of tasteful melodies, tunes were embellished with every species of superfluous ornament; so much so that Aristophanes was constrained to point out that in the time of his forefathers measured rhythm and simple melody were the fundamental rules of music. True, many modern writers have expressed the same sentiments relative to the music of *their* forefathers; nevertheless, it is obvious from other evidence collected, that *Zopf* had become a feature of Greek music—that word used to express the degenerate phase of art—when mere *embellishment* predominates in contradistinction to *substance*. "Thus artifice was substituted for art, and sensuous effect for heartfelt emotion."[5]

With so radical a change in their music, the character of the Greeks themselves weakened; their *morale* declined; their military enterprises were unsuccessful; they allowed other nations to meddle in their affairs; finally, they lost their patriotism and love of independence, and, with the loss of these, prosperity was at an end.

It is instructive to note that music gradually began to fall from its elevated status at the very period at which the other Greek arts had attained their greatest excellence, namely, during the era of Pericles, 444 to 429 BCE. If the reverse had been the case, there would be some grounds for the proverbial notion that a particular type of music is the result of character, morals, and so forth, instead of vice versa; or that when the other arts flourish, so does music along with them. But the Greek writers knew otherwise; for even apart from that esoteric knowledge, which Plato, for one, undoubtedly possessed, history enforced the lesson that the rise and decay of the tonal art was most intimately connected with the rise and decay of civilisation itself.

30

The Romans and Their Music

Whereas Greece fell through a perverted love of beauty, Rome fell through a perverted love of manliness.

It has been said, and rightly so, that the Romans were the most practical people in history; they were a people of action, but not of imagination. Like the matter-of-fact downright type of Englishman, they admired manliness, self-restraint, seriousness of demeanour, industry, and the natural outcome of these: Law and Order. Of the subtler qualities they had little or no understanding; their art was realistic, their architecture massive, and their attitude towards religion mostly material. They were a people of high military talent who by their "simplicity, veracity, and by their sober unimaginativeness had conquered an empire and governed it in a way which constitutes the most important epoch in the history of the world."[1]

Yet the time was to come when Rome was to be celebrated not for its greatness, but for its unprecedented depravity. Let us seek to discover if music played any part in its rise and decline, and if so, to what extent. Sir John Hawkins writes:

> If we enquire into the state of music among the Romans, we shall
> find that as a science, they held it in small estimation . . . it only

169

serves to show the low state of Roman music when the best instruments they could find to celebrate the praises of their deities were a few sorry pipes, little better than those we now offer as playthings for children.[2]

It is thus obvious that there was little music in Rome; there was, however, one type which for purely utilitarian reasons the Romans did encourage, and that was martial music; for it added its quota to the making of fine soldiers. And it was not limited to "a few sorry pipes. . . ." There is evidence to show that "the Romans possessed an unusually large number of martial and especially of wind instruments,"[3] the chief of this kind being the Tuba and Buccina. The former was somewhat like a trumpet, though much larger and longer than the modern orchestral trumpet; the latter was somewhat like a horn, though again much larger than our modern horn.

To give a detailed account of the effects of this martial music; it energised the body and tended to produce health, courage, and sex—virility—those qualities, which make up the one composite quality that the Romans called *virtus,* or manliness, as the word finally came to signify. It was, in fact, an entirely restricted type of music, with correspondingly restricted effects: it worked upon the physical, yet, owing to its lack of the more mellow phases, it engendered no love of physical beauty as the Greeks understood it, for it did not touch those emotions that inspire imagination. Whereas the Greeks admired a powerful healthy body because they considered it beautiful, the Romans admired it because they considered it useful; the one point of view was aesthetic, the other practical; the basis of both standpoints was the physical, but the angles from which it was regarded were widely divergent.

Now, the effects of martial music pure and simple, unless counteracted by more refining influences, are liable, in the course of time, to become detrimental to character; manliness may degenerate into love of power, courage into brutality, and sex: virility into sensualism. And this is precisely what occurred with the Romans. The Revolution of 133 BCE was due to the first-mentioned of these bad qualities; it was

entirely the result "of an antagonism between the few who possessed
the reins of power and the many who conceived they had a right to that
possession." As to the second of the evils enumerated we find it in its
most virulent form in those terrible Gladiatorial Games, which came to
be a feature of the later days of Roman society, and which were excused
on the plea "that they upheld the military spirit by the constant spectacle of courageous death." Whether they temporarily sustained that spirit
or not, they were largely responsible for the downfall of Rome, which
has been shown by historians; for they took such a hold on the nation
that all else was neglected. Apart from the fact that these games encouraged inhumanity, they encouraged idleness, having become of such
absorbing interest to the people that the various industrial occupations
were set aside, together with those others that go to the maintenance of
the State. But if brutality played havoc with the nation, sensualism, the
third vice we have mentioned, proved equally destructive. Sensualism
and its concomitant dissipation, owing to the weakening effect they
have upon the body and nerves, are very frequently provocative of cowardice, and when there is an epidemic of cowardice in a State it stands
at the mercy of its enemies. Indifference is substituted for patriotism,
and the people cease to care whether they are ruled by their own coun-
trymen or by foreign invaders.

The foregoing were thus the effects of martial music: the exact
opposite of those intended. Nevertheless, Rome might have been saved
if another musical ingredient could have been added to its potion: the
best features of Greek music before it degenerated into mere virtuosity.
As most people are aware, when the Romans conquered Greece there
was a considerable influx of Greek literature into Rome, but although
a certain amount of music was borne along with it, the Roman musical
taste was such that the better class was never accepted in Roman society; in fact, the love of the virtuoso was even more pronounced than it
had come to be in Greece. Moreover, writes Naumann:

It is a question whether the Roman *virtuosi* were not more admired
for their personal blandishments and enchantments than for their

skilful performances. In place of one celebrated female flautist, as in Greece, Rome possessed whole groups of them. The story of the degenerate and degraded citharoedes and female flautists is a dark page in the history of Rome. The decay of the tonal art was so complete, its practice falling into the hands of adventurous strangers and women who enticed by their charms, that, by the direction of the State, it was expunged from the curriculum of Roman education, the State arguing that an art practiced by slaves and the despised classes of society was not befitting to the educational training of youthful patricians. Thus, all too soon, were fulfilled the prophetic words of Aristotle, that an art having for its object the mere display of manual skill and sensuous attraction was unbecoming to the dignity of men, and fit only for slaves.[4]

The above requires little comment, for it is self-evident that a music lacking in such essentials would not only be powerless to counteract the baneful effects of a preponderance of martial music, but, in view of what has been stated in the last chapter, would cause a further degeneracy in the national character.

31

Effects of Descant and the Folk Song

"'Tis agreed of all the learned that the science of music so admired by the ancients is wholly lost, and that what we have now is made up of certain notes that fell into the fancy or observation of a poor friar in chanting his *matins*." Thus quaintly wrote Alypius, who lived ca. 115 CE, for with the decline of Greece and Rome, music in Europe practically died out. In any case it was of so limited a type that we find no historical reference to it worthy of mention until the days of St. Ambrose, 374 CE, when the Western churches adopted the practice of singing at their services.

This introduction of a certain form in primitive church music was not without its result; through the constant repetition of single tones, with occasional deviations to lower or higher ones, a chant of a *mantramistic* nature was produced, which had a direct influence on the brain, because it inclined men to think in a more orderly manner. And as the majority of souls incarnate at that time were young and unevolved, and hence possessed of undeveloped mentalities, this was highly essential. Only by using the brain is the *mental body* formed and nourished; a fact we have already pointed out. As disorderly thinking by the force of habit produces disorderly minds, an external agent had to be employed; that agent was the Ambrosian Chant.

That it compelled the congregation while singing it to *pay attention*—for it forced them to concentrate their minds—gave it already a certain power, but, in addition, it had more subtle effects; it was partly instrumental in eventually inspiring the clergy to introduce a method of ceremonial into the Church that had not been previously employed.

Although from the times of St. Ambrose, music had somewhat tended to develop the minds of Christians, no innovation worthy of mention was connected with it until about two centuries later, when St. Gregory the Great became pope. As the Ambrosian Chant had been limited to four modes, he increased them to eight; and this resulted in the institution of what is termed "plain song," or the Gregorian Chant. This acted as an aid to devotion, and rendered the minds of the whole congregation one-pointed. It also tended to calm the emotions, and so gave a measure of control over the *emotional body.* For one thing it was, musically speaking, too austere to arouse those pleasant feelings, which true melody arouses; for another, when the mind is fully engaged, the emotions—at any rate the more turbulent ones—are usually for the time being quiescent; and we say advisedly "for the time being," because it took a very considerable period of years before mankind in general acquired a measure of control over their emotions. If we study life in the Middle Ages, with its sensuality and cruel fanaticism, we find lack of emotional, or, better said, passional control to be the root of all its vices. Although the Gregorian chant is still sung in some churches, its influence is now very much limited, and only a certain type of unsophisticated mind responds to its vibrations. The appeal, which it may make to others, is due to their own respect for tradition rather than to its inherent value as music. Indeed, until Guido of Arrezzo, born in 990, made his innovations, all European music was still so circumscribed and attenuated that only its "mediaeval flavour" has saved it from complete oblivion. For Guido was the first European composer to use chords in such a way that they sound harmonious.

The effects of his music were considerable, for it was instrumental in helping to bring harmonious relations into the home and social life. How this was accomplished is again explained by that law of correspondences: as in music, so in life. In all compositions where there are chords or more than one voice, or part, there must perforce exist that coherence, which naturally connotes law and order, in a word, coordination. Chordal music, in fact, is the musical prototype of harmonious relationships between individual units, and its effect is to produce a feeling of friendliness. And, of course, if in addition it is associated with religion; the result is friendliness plus religious devotion. It was the instinctive recognition of this truth that resulted in the introduction of hymns into the Church service. But these effects of chordal music, especially that of Guido's, were not limited to social relationships; they also to some extent harmonized the *mental* and emotional organisms, thus producing greater unity between them. Henceforward, man was no longer to be an absolute slave of his emotions, but to begin to experience the domination of the mind; the two were in some small measure to be brought into alignment; they were to work more in conjunction instead of at variance.

The harmonisation of the mind and emotions had a further result; it was conducive to the production of *art*. Only when the emotions and the mind are conjoined can any form of art worthy of the name be created; for although the inspirational impulse usually comes through the emotions, the mind is responsible for the technique. Thus, Guido's music paved the way for that great school of art, which commenced with the advent of Cimabue around 1280.

From the tenth to the thirteenth century, when Feudalism reached its zenith, and when the effects of Guido's music had become fully operative, we meet with a variety of noble sentiments, further inspired by that type of folk song known as that of the Troubadours. These latter, with their graceful melodies and quaint lyrical conceits, while on the one hand they fostered heroism, on the other hand fostered the "gentler side of life," known by the name of *Chivalry*. Indeed, the combination of the Troubadour song and its variants was, in conjunction with the devotion-inspiring church music, responsible for the

Knight-errant and the Crusader: in the latter both religion and love
of adventure were combined. The Crusades, however, were especially
significant in view of what we have previously written, since they were
the first enterprise in which the whole of Europe took part, and hence
were another external sign of coordination.

32

Polyphony and Its Effects

We have now to consider an important innovation in musical device that occurred as early as the thirteenth century; it is technically known as *canon,* a word derived from the Greek *Kavcp,* meaning "rule" or "standard." According to *Grove's Dictionary:*

> Its principle is that one voice begins a melody, which melody is imitated precisely, note for note, and (generally) interval for interval, by some other voice, either at the same or a different pitch, beginning a few notes later, and thus, as it were, running after the leader. . . . Often in a quartet there may be a *canon* between two of the voices, while the other two are free, or three voices may be in *canon,* and the fourth part free.

The effects of *canon* and *imitation* considerably enhanced those inspired by the chordal music mentioned in our last chapter; they were conducive to an easier give-and-take in human intercourse, as may again be perceived by the law of correspondences. For the *canon* itself is formed on the principle of give-and-take; the melody being first sung by one voice, then by another, while, in the case of a quartet, the two remaining voices fill in the harmony. But the *canon,* as well as all other forms

177

of polyphonic music, tends—owing to its mathematical qualities—to develop the intellect;* and hence we find that the more polyphonic music became, the more noticeable those attributes that went to the forming of what Draper has termed the "Age of Reason."

From the *canon* was developed that well-known and elaborate form of music known as the fugue. This "species of symphoniac composition, in which a certain . . . subject is propounded by one part and prosecuted by another," exercised such a marked effect on the mentality that by degrees more and more people began to use their reasoning powers in every direction. They were no longer content to accept without question the misdemeanours of the clergy or such religious tenets as tradition had handed down. They found flaws in this and that argument, they objected to this and that doctrine, and so the Reformation and Protestantism, and eventually a large number of other religious movements, came into being.

---

*This we mentioned when dealing with Bach's music, which was the culmination of the polyphonic style.

33

Music and the Reformation

The Reformation, as everyone knows, engendered manifold consequences; for one thing, by causing a general circulation of religious creeds, "it awoke religion amidst the laity." Hitherto, it had been entirely in the hands of the priests; they alone were permitted to teach and preach it; but *after* the Reformation a decided change occurred, and religion became, as it were, common property. Laymen discussed it; laymen—if they felt so inclined—taught and preached it. Yet even in spite of the Reformation, religion would not have played such an important part in the lives of a number of people had there not been other agencies at work.

During the course of a hundred years there were three composers born who exercised a marked effect on the spiritual-emotional nature of those sensitive enough to respond. The first of these composers was Orlandus Lassus, otherwise called Orlando de Lasso, a native of Mons, in Hainault, he lived from 1522 to 1595. The second was Palestrina, 1529 to 1594; and the third was Monteverde, who flourished around 1600.

Of Orlando de Lasso it has been said:

He was the first great improver of figurative music, for instead of adhering to that stiff formal rule of counterpoint, from which some

179

of his predecessors seemed afraid to deviate, he gave way to the introduction of elegant points and responsive passages finely wrought.[1]

In more modern words, he endowed music with what is termed
appeal, and in so doing was the first European composer to give
Mankind a glimpse of the spiritual through the emotions. By his music
he so influenced the emotional nature of those who responded to it,
that they aspired to the attainment of pure Devotion, or what is termed
God-like Love.* And we say advisedly *aspired,* for it is one thing to yearn
towards the spiritual planes and another thing to reach them. That specific music calculated to induce Cosmic or God-consciousness has so
far not appeared in Europe, though the creations of Richard Wagner
were a step towards it, as we have already seen.

As implied, Palestrina and Monteverde continued the work that
Orlando de Lasso had commenced. That the music of Palestrina deeply
touched the heart and elevated the mind is obvious from the eulogies he
called forth from contemporary writers. We find him referred to as "a
great genius . . . who adopted a style . . . so elegant, so noble, so learned,
and so pleasing and . . . whose works breathe such divine harmony" that
they inspired people to sing in a "manner truly sublime the praises of
God." Thus, it will be seen that not only was there a spiritual quality in the
music of Palestrina which, combined with its polyphonic qualities, urged
people to *think,* but owing to its effect on the higher emotional nature, to
think in a more spiritual way: it was their emotions, which, so to speak,
directed the course of their thought. The German historian Ranke even
implies that Palestrina's music—the Mass composed in 1560—had almost
immediate results; it revived religion and instituted an epoch of devotion.

Lasso, Palestrina, and finally Monteverde—whose work we need
not analyze in view of its similarity of effect—were, through their
music, instrumental in preparing the way for a certain number of mystics, poets and philosophers who appeared after the sixteenth century.

---

*The reader is reminded that Indian music brought about a somewhat similar effect, not
via the emotions, but by a subtilisation of the *mind.*

34

The Music of the Seventeenth and Eighteenth Centuries

All music-lovers are familiar with the works of Domenico Scarlatti, born 1685, died 1757. He is described as the greatest solo performer on the harpsichord of his period, a description, which may well be true, judging from the large number of *bravura* works he wrote for that instrument. Among his other achievements he is credited with "perfecting the Sonata form," which hitherto had been restricted almost entirely to works for the violin; but as to this, it were more correct to say that he greatly improved it, seeing that even with Beethoven it had not reached the limit of its potentialities.

The effect of Scarlatti's charming rippling music must be so apparent to those who have heard any of his compositions that only a few words on the subject seem necessary. They induce a feeling of gaiety and exhilaration and also tend to make us mentally more alert. Yet as we of today only hear them on the pianoforte and not on the harpsichord, for which they were composed, much of their original effect is lost. The gaiety remains but the "sting" is absent; for whereas the metal strings of the harpsichord were plucked, on the piano they are struck by felt-covered hammers.

To appreciate fully the effects of the harpsichord one need only compare them with those of the church organ. The latter, with its solemn sustained tones, immediately tends to provoke reverence and religious devotion, the former with its sharp metallic twang, emotions well-nigh exactly the reverse—instead of reverence, light-heartedness and humour, instead of religious devotion, causticity, and satire. Thus the harpsichord, clavecin, and spinet, in short, any instrument in which metallic strings were *plucked,* tended, especially when employed for florid sparkling music, to the increase of mordant wit and brilliance. It is to the above-mentioned instruments, or rather to their effects upon the mind, that we owe much of that generous legacy of eighteenth-century sharp-pointed humour to be found in greater abundance in the works of Voltaire, and to a lesser degree in those of his contemporaries. As already stated, polyphonic music, *per se* stimulates the intellect; add to polyphony "effervescence," scintillation, and the stinging effects of plucked strings, and the result is intellect employed in caustic utterance, or satirical wit. Indeed, after the disappearance of the harpsichord, that particular type of satirical wit also began to diminish.*

With the advent of the pianoforte and its mellower tone, a less caustic type of humour came into being; it had lost its specific "bite," whatever other characteristics it may still have retained.

Scarlatti's music, as such, cannot be said to have had an influence on the nation as a whole, but although its effects were limited they were perhaps more immediate than those of any musician we have previously examined. It is a general rule that the more facile and exhilarating a type of music, the more immediate, and also ephemeral, its effects. For this reason we find that all those tuneful, hence easily comprehensible, clavecin and harpsichord composers, whom we need not enumerate, but of whom Scarlatti was the most "fluent," exercised *en masse* an almost immediate effect upon their epoch, whereas Beethoven's music, for example, took about a hundred years to reach the plenitude of its influence.

---

*The less biting species to be found in the celebrated French *Salons* was much influenced by the graceful dance-forms written under the title of *Suites for Clavecin,* by "Couperin le Grand," as he was called. He was born in 1668 and died in 1733.

Bearing in mind, then, the comparatively rapid results of the more superficial music, we shall understand the partial causes of that phase of life, that effeminacy in male attire and manners, which was so pronounced a feature of the eighteenth century. Already during the lifetime of Scarlatti, we find the commencement in the tonal art of *Zopf,* which, as already stated relative to Greece, means the elaboration of one side of artistic activity at the expense of all others . . . "the predominance of the unreal, the incidental, and external over the real, the essential, the internal."[1] Its insignia in music are shakes, runs, and variations; its insignia in life are affectations, adornment, "bowings and scrapings" and "frills and furbelows." Nor have we far to seek for its underlying cause: it is the "gentler side of life" carried to extremes and degenerated almost to caricature. Musically speaking, it began with the romantic type of folk song, was elaborated in the days of Scarlatti, and reached its culmination in the works of Mozart, (1756–1791). Indeed, with the exception of J. S. Bach and Handel,* nearly all the composers who wrote from the time of Scarlatti to that of Mozart were through their works responsible either for the elaboration of "the gentler side of life," or for the increase of wit, as already mentioned. But Mozart actually *expressed* that gentler side in terms of music; nay, more; he was the musical interpreter par excellence of all the little vanities of the daily round, as was also his contemporary, Joseph Haydn.† The two were in many ways so similar that it is unnecessary to study them separately, as far as the purpose of this book is concerned. They were even alike in the immediate fame they acquired for themselves, seeing that after the production of *Idomeneo,* Mozart was hailed as the "greatest of all musicians," while Haydn "caused the utmost possible excitement" among the English musical public when he produced six of his "Twelve Grand Symphonies" in 1791.

Yet—startling contrast—just two years before Joseph Haydn was enthralling London audiences by his exhilarating "vanities," the French Revolution commenced, and three years later the prisons were broken

---

*See *ante.*

†This does not apply to his cantatas, but to his symphonic, chamber music, and so forth. The *Creation* and the *Seasons* had a somewhat similar effect to Handel's works.

open and twelve thousand persons, including a hundred priests, were massacred. It is evident, therefore, that in France, at any rate, forces were at work which that no amount of "immediately fascinating" music was capable of counteracting. Now, if we turn to French musical history, we find the significant fact that towards the end of the Renaissance period a remarkable change had taken place in France. Where previously "Church music had reigned supreme, organists, choirboys, trained to chant *a capella* song, were supplanted by singers who performed their roles in the costliest of garments, and by dancers decked out in multicoloured ribbons, accompanied by an orchestra of profane instruments."[2] Thus there finally came a day when although in Italy the elevating Masses of Alessandro Scarlatti* were disseminating religion, in France the tinkling and contrastingly frivolous strains of the clavecin composers were merely inspiring caustic wit and satirical brilliance. But even prior to this, the eminent Giovanni Battista Lulli, a Tuscan by birth who resided in Paris, had spread abroad the worldly effects of his many pleasing and tuneful sarabandes, courantes, and gigues.

We see, then, that the church music in France, which at one time had inspired religious thinking, had practically disappeared, and with its disappearance thought had become diverted into other channels: either the very reverse of religious, or, still worse, religious only in name, but mundane and despotic in actuality. The result was a conflict between a sincere scepticism and an insincere Church, a conflict in which, on the one side, all the notable writers arrayed themselves to attempt the overthrow of "spiritual" despotism, and, on the other, the clergy fought to retain the power they were loth to renounce. Yet that was only the first stage in the conflict; the second was the attempt of subsequent notable writers to overthrow secular despotism, the ultimate outcome being the Revolution.

---

*Domenico's father is especially noted for the appealing type of Masses he composed.

35

$\mathscr{A}$ Cursory View of Musical Effects in England

from the Pre-Elizabethan Days to Those of Handel

When we speak of some man of genius as being the product of a particular age, we are uttering what is but superficially true. Those who accept the doctrine of reincarnation know that a genius is the finished product of an entire series of past lives, and that if he is born in a particular age it is because the Higher Powers and his own ego so decreed. The age is, as it were, but the soil in which he may thrive or wilt according to his *karma*. The effects of music may be instrumental in preparing that soil, but of course we do not claim that they can produce genius itself. This must be borne in mind now that we come to consider those musical influences that operated prior to the birth of Shakespeare.

It will be remembered that the invention of polyphony gave a very considerable impetus to the mental faculties, and that, broadly speaking, if employed in the composition of solemn pieces, it induced serious thinking, and if in lighter pieces, "cleverness" and wit. A marked advance was made in both secular and sacred polyphonic music until about 1450, then there came a period of weakness until about 1480, when a prodigious evolution in three kinds of music took place, viz. in church music (solemn), madrigals (varied, i.e., both grave and gay), chamber-music (light and pleasing). In the latter type the virginal* was employed: a plucked metal-stringed instrument that preceded the invention of the harpsichord; it was less powerful than the harpsichord, but nevertheless produced some of the same effects. Other instruments employed were lutes and viols, usually to be found in sets corresponding to alto, tenor, and bass. And it does not require a great effort of the imagination to realize their effect. With their mellow, rather sensuous tones, they awoke the more poetic sentiments in the heart; while, in conjunction with the plucked strings of the lute and virginal, they inspired "cleverness," and hence the production of those "pretty conceits" that are so marked a feature of nearly all lyrical poetry. As to the madrigals, whether grave or gay, who has not experienced the effects of their quaint graceful melodiousness when sung by the Oriana choir?

To summarize: first and foremost we have Church music, productive of Thought in the higher sense of the word, and its results—drama, philosophy, and so forth—then the madrigals, inspiring either grace, gaiety or "sweet sadness"; and, finally, we have the chamber-music, inspiring wit and poetic sentiments. Combine all these elements and we realise whence arose the Elizabethan age, with its array of playwrights, poets, its brilliance, happiness, and monumental productivity. Nor in making this statement are we overlooking the large part played by the influence of Italy during this era: Italy, with its poetry and romances, its manners and customs. That the literature of Italy, that even its picturesque dress and speech, "became objects of almost passionate admiration"[1] is well known. As no amount of bril-

---

*It has been supposed that the virginal was so termed after Elizabeth, the "Virgin Queen" because she was a skilled performer on it, but, as it is mentioned under that name in manuscripts pre-dating her epoch, the supposition is not tenable.

liance in others can transform a dullard into a savant, so no amount of brilliance in Italy* could have transformed the English into what they were during the Elizabethan epoch.

We have now to deal with an instrument, which has exercised a marked influence on the people of this country for several centuries, namely the organ. There is ample historical evidence to show that already in 951 a huge organ was built at Winchester, and that by the time of Henry VII there must have been a large number of organs—though comparatively small ones—to be found all over England. The spiritual effect of this instrument is that of bringing the Unseen nearer to the human heart; it constitutes, as it were, a bridge between the world of matter and the world of Spirit. The more obvious effects, however, are to induce an atmosphere of austere grandeur, of exalted magnificence. But this, of course, applies to the elaborate organs capable of producing an enormous volume of sound; the effect of the small species, on the other hand, is to induce that austere religiosity or piety that comes under the heading of Puritanism.

If we dismiss for a moment what has been said about the madrigals and the Elizabethan chamber-music and their influence, and try to imagine the state of mind of any person who heard and desired to hear nothing but organ music, we must perforce imagine a very one-sided personality. Although he might be serene and contented, he would be averse to anything in the form of gaiety or the harmless frivolities of life. If he loved the beautiful, it would be the severe type, the sombre-hued grandeur: the type which inspired reverence and awe, but not exhilaration and felicitous love. Now although it is safe to say that hardly a person exists who has heard no other music than that of the organ, there are some who admit that alone the "king of instruments," as they call it, has the power to move them: such persons obviously existed in the time of Henry VIII. They will have heard the charming madrigals, and the equally charming chamber-music, but to neither of these did they

---

*Some historians mentioned France, not Italy, but whether it was the one or the other, or both, is immaterial so far as our argument is concerned.

respond; only sacred music affected their austere natures, only to sacred music did their emotional organisms vibrate.

We have already implied elsewhere that the same cause does not always produce the same effect, and in the subject under consideration we find a further instance of this truth. The musical agency, which induces profound philosophical speculation of a spiritual nature in one temperament, may merely induce religious austerity and Puritanism in another. It is partly for this reason that the beginnings of Puritanism arose in an otherwise non-Puritanical age: the rest may be understood from history. For it is known that the Puritans influenced the Church and Society from within, not from without, and only became a political power when the offence of Charles I against the Constitution compelled them to oppose force to force. And if it be asked why the Puritanical spirit eventually took such a hold upon the nation, the answer is that it was but a temporary hold, and, for the most part, actuated by political motives. It was owing to this that the gay influences of the secular music were for the time being impotent to counteract it. That it might have lasted longer if the Puritan forces had pursued a different policy we do not doubt; but, strange irony, they suppressed the very forces which moulded and sustained the whole movement. Instead of suppressing the secular, they suppressed the church music,[*2] and especially the use of organs. The result was that during the whole of the Commonwealth, anti-Puritan music was spreading its influence abroad. Thus the psychological moment alone was needed for it to come into fullest manifestation: that moment was when Charles II entered Whitehall. It was then that the extraordinary revulsion of feeling occurred that proved that the Puritanical movement had been a superimposed condition and not an inherent necessity of the national heart.

Everyone knows the state of society after the fall of the Puritans. Yet, in order to emphasise the results, which accrued after the sobering influences of the organ and Church music had been suppressed and

---

[*]It has been conclusively proved that the Commonwealth was a most brilliant period for secular music.

the lighter type had full sway, we may quote a sentence from Green's *History*. "Duelling and raking," he wrote, "became the marks of a fine gentleman: and grave divines winked at the follies of 'honest fellows' who fought, gambled, swore, drank, and ended a day of debauchery by a night in the gutter."

The perverted gaiety of the times, however, was in part responsible for one significant resolve—that of re-establishing musical services in the churches. No longer were the people content with the unspeakable gloominess of worship without the adjunct of the organ and choir; and so among other institutions we find that the Corporation of Music, which Charles I had established, was again set up. We also find during this period the names of several composers associated with the composition of sacred and organ music. But especially should that of Henry Purcell be noted, not only on account of his genius, but because of the soberising effect his work came to have upon the nation.

The characteristics of Purcell's style may easily be summed up: he contrived in a masterly fashion to add "the sweetness of Italian melody to the severer beauty of Elizabethan counterpoint." Thus, at one and the same time his music stirred the gentler emotions and affected the mentality. Indeed, his sacred compositions, of which there were a large number, had much the same effect upon the English people as had those of Alessandro Scarlatti upon the Italians: they served to render religion more attractive. It is related that "whenever Purcell's 'Te Deum' was performed, the church was packed to overflowing," a circumstance that requires no comment. There was in Purcell's music an element, which delighted its hearers, and, at the same time, aroused in them a certain measure of awe. Listening to that combination of voices, orchestra, and organ, which in his larger works he employed, they felt as if under the spell of something religiously magnificent. It is therefore Purcell to whom one must give a meed of credit for those characteristics of the Victorian age for which Handel's influence was so largely responsible.

PART V
Some Occult Prognostications
Toward Beauty and Mystery

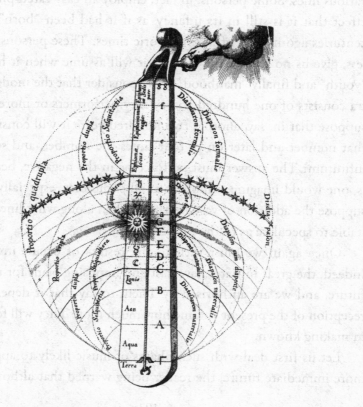

36

The Music of
the Future

The future of music is a subject that invites much speculation along various lines. Some persons, in fact, employ an easy catch-phrase to the effect that it is still in its infancy, as if it had been "born" some few centuries ago instead of in prehistoric times. These persons, nevertheless, give us no clue to the features it will assume when it has reached "youth" and finally "manhood." If we consider that the modern orchestra consists of one hundred and twenty performers or more, are we to suppose that in, say, another two hundred years it will consist of twice that number and later on of four times the number, and so forth, ad infinitum? The answer must perforce be in the negative, because there is, one would imagine, a limit to aural endurance, especially if we presuppose the addition of vast choruses. Then along what lines is it profitable to speculate as to the musical future?

Once again we must turn to the results of occult investigation. Indeed, the great Initiates have vast and imposing plans for the musical future, and we are authorised by Them to say that it depends on the reception of the present volume how much more They will feel justified in making known.

Let us first deal with such phases of music likely to appear in the more immediate future, the reader being warned that although we can naturally only treat of each one in succession, some of them may be operating concurrently.

For the next decade or so, the prevailing note of serious music will tend to be unemotional and intellectual in character,[1] and although here and there composers far ahead of their time may be "reaching out towards that Beauty and Mystery, which are veritably as the garments of God,"[2] such composers will not receive their due until a much later date, nay, perhaps only after their death.

Meanwhile, as everyone is aware, we are much troubled by the nerve-shattering noise to which in all large towns we are subjected, and which, far from decreasing, is only likely to increase as time goes on. The jarring sounds of motor-horns, whistles, grinding brakes, and so forth exercise a cumulative and deleterious effect upon the entire organism. In order to help to counteract this, certain composers will be used to evolve a type of music calculated to heal where these discordant noises have destroyed. For this end, of course, etheric vision or, at any rate, great inner sensitiveness, will be indispensable, so that the value of each combination of notes and its effect upon the subtler vehicles of the listeners may be fully realised.[3] Such men, consciously aware of their responsibility towards humanity, will indeed be as faithful custodians of the sacred two-edged sword of Sound.

Certain gifted composers will further set themselves the task of writing types of music creating thought-forms suited to specific moods or emotional states. With the vast array of musical resources available, they will be able to meet the needs of the most complex of modern psychology.

Again, music in the future is to be used to bring people into yet closer touch with the Devas; they will be enabled to partake of the benefic influence of these beings while attending concerts at which by the appropriate type of sound they have been invoked. Although at the present time music is extant, which calls forth the Devas or nature-spirits, the ordinary listener is not conscious of their presence, and thus there is no actual rapport between the members of the two evolutions. The scientifically calculated music in question however will achieve the twofold object of invoking the Devas and at the same time stimulating in the listeners those faculties by means of which they will become aware of them and responsive to their influence. Among these Devas will be those especially concerned with the animal kingdom. The result will be a revolt against that form of cruelty called blood-sports. Efforts are already (1958) being made to bring in a law to prohibit such sports. Further, in the course of time, music will become more and more potent to bring humanity into touch with the higher planes, thus enabling them to experience a spiritual joy and exaltation that now can only be experienced by the very few.

Having thus dealt, albeit cursorily, with the esoteric side of the music of the future, we will now give an indication of some of its more apparent characteristics.

Innovations will take place in connection with concerts. Already there have been complaints from the more fastidious music lovers that concert halls are too garishly lighted, and that what is seen detracts from what is heard. Such people, however, have usually been set down as cranks, and concert promoters have paid no heed to their idiosyncrasies. Nevertheless, the time will come when the demands of these so-called cranks will be fulfilled, and in an atmosphere of semi-darkness colours of every variety will be projected onto a screen, expressive of and corresponding to the content of the music. Thus, will that dream of Scriabin's be realised (see chapter 21): the unity of colour and sound; and through its realisation the audiences of the future will experience the healing and stimulating effects of that very potent conjunction.

Meanwhile the discordant element of the present day will have made way for concord; and melody, without which no music can long survive the dust of time, will have been reinstated. As the music of the last twenty-five years has in so large a measure been disruptive in character, the music we may anticipate in the future will be constructive.

From among other information conveyed, we gather that America will be particularly responsive to this new music, for that great continent is the cradle of the coming race, the units of which, in common with the majority of artistic types, will function through the sympathetic system in contradistinction to the cerebro-spinal. The enthusiasm and the keen receptivity to new ideas which already constitute such a marked characteristic of the more sensitive Americans of today, make them peculiarly appreciative of novel combinations of sound. From among them many famous executants will be born, some of whom will exhibit great proficiency on a new species of violin to be invented in the future. On this violin it will be possible to convey the more subtle divisions of the tone, and to draw from it the maximum of its potentialities will necessitate on the part of the performer an even greater degree of musical sensitivity than at the present time.

We have been living in the Age of Destruction when, as stated earlier, even ultra-discordant music has been used to destroy certain baneful thought-forms. This type of music, however, has served its purpose already some years ago, and it is now for Concord to rebuild.

"As above, so below . . ." Just as the denizens of the earth who represent cells in the body of the great Planetary Logos have gone through the purifying fires of two world-wars, so on a much mightier and to us incomprehensible scale has that Logos Himself also passed through the fire, and is now in process of taking a higher Initiation that must inevitably affect each unit within His consciousness. New cosmic currents of force are beginning to circulate throughout His aura, inspiring new and harmonious qualities, tendencies, and ideals; and it will be the exalted function of music to help to focus these currents and further their rhythmic distribution. Great floods of melody will be poured forth from the higher planes, to be translated into earthly sound by composers sensitive enough to apprehend them. At first only a faint echo of these melodies will penetrate the spheres of human endeavour, and the music of the next few decades can only be, as it were, a prelude to what will follow.

The National Devas of various countries, working through Sound, will seek to form a bridge between nations by inspiring the harmony of true co-operation and that genuine peace which that is not merely the laying down of arms. Through them a new form of patriotism will be inspired, the spirit of which when voiced will be, "How can my country contribute to the international good?" Instead of "How can my country show itself superior to others?" Thus, in place of the old type of martial national anthem, a type will be substituted that will urge the nations towards the realisation of Brotherhood. Already at long last they are beginning to recognise that the form of separateness, which masquerades under the name of Nationalism, is as unprofitable as, to the few enlightened, it is unspiritual.[4] And so the day is drawing nigh when it will be rejected for the purely material reason that it does not pay. This attitude, of course, falls far short of the ideal, which the Great Ones are ever seeking to put before humanity, for only when true Brotherhood is felt in the heart will that ideal be attained.

To this end the great World Teacher, The Christ, will come again; though exactly when He will come must largely depend on Humanity itself and better relations between the Powers. There is hope that He may come at the close of the century. But when He does come it will be to inspire, to construct, to "make all things new." And it will be for music, by creating harmony within Man's subtler bodies, to make ready for and facilitate His advent.

Yet even then music will not have reached the limit of its potentialities. So far, with our earthly music we have only been able to imitate the faintest echo of the Music of the Spheres, but in the future it will be given us to swell the great Cosmic Symphony. In that unimaginable Unity-Song is the synthesis of Love, Wisdom, Knowledge, and Joy, and when Man shall have heard it upon earth and become imbued with its divine influence he will attain the eternal consciousness of all these attributes.

I am able to conclude this edition of the book with a recently received message from the Master K. H. It is:

Today, as we enter this new Age, we seek, primarily through the medium of *inspired* music, to diffuse the spirit of unification and brotherhood, and thus quicken the vibration of this planet.

Notes

CHAPTER 4. INSPIRED AND UNINSPIRED COMPOSERS

1. Abell, *Talks with Great Composers.*

CHAPTER 5. THE ESOTERIC SOURCE OF THIS BOOK

1. Besant, *Mahatma Letters to A. P. Sinnett.*
2. Anrias, *Through the Eyes of the Masters.*
3. See Schuré, *The Initiate,* etc.

CHAPTER 7. GEORGE FREDERICK HANDEL AND THE VICTORIAN ERA

1. Ramsey, *The Genius of Handel.*
2. Crotch, *Lectures on Music.*
3. Ibid.
4. Ramsey, *The Genius of Handel.*
5. Rolland, *Handel.*

CHAPTER 8. COMPARISON BETWEEN THE INFLUENCE OF HANDEL AND BACH

1. Naumann, *History of Music.*
2. Ibid.

3. Ibid.
4. *Grove's Dictionary of Music and Musicians.*

CHAPTER 9. BEETHOVEN, SYMPATHY AND PSYCHOANALYSIS

1. See *Grove's Dictionary.*
2. Ibid.
3. Ibid.

CHAPTER 10. THE MENDELSSOHNIAN SYMPATHY

1. Rockstro, *Mendelssohn.*
2. Ibid.
3. Hiller, *Mendelssohn.*

CHAPTER 11. FREDERIC CHOPIN, THE APOSTLE OF REFINEMENT

1. See Niecks, *The Life of Chopin* vol. II, p. 322.
2. See Huneker, *Chopin.*
3. Ibid.
4. See Niecks, *The Life of Chopin.*
5. Ibid.
6. Ibid.
7. Huneker, *Chopin.*
8. Ibid.
9. See Tarnowski, *Chopin: As Revealed by Extracts from His Diary.*
10. See Mendelssohn's *Letters from Italy.*
11. See Liszt, *Life of Chopin.*

CHAPTER 12. CHOPIN, THE PRE-RAPHAELITES, AND THE EMANCIPATION OF WOMEN

1. Liszt, *Life of Chopin.*

CHAPTER 13. ROBERT SCHUMANN AND THE CHILD-NATURE

1. See Fisher, *The Montessori Manual.*
2. See *Grove's Dictionary.*
3. See Hadow, *Studies in Modern Music.*

4. Ibid.

5. See *Grove's Dictionary*, Schumann.

6. Ibid.

7. See Hadow, *Studies in Modern Music*.

CHAPTER 14. THE EFFECTS OF WAGNER'S MUSIC

1. See Hadow, *Studies in Modern Music*.

2. Ibid.

3. Lidgey, *Wagner*.

4. Ibid.

CHAPTER 16. MUSICIANS AND THE HIGHER POWERS

1. Challoner, *Watchers of the Seven Spheres*.

CHAPTER 17. THE OCCULT CONSTITUTION OF MAN

1. See Hinton, *The Fourth Dimension*.

CHAPTER 18. CÉSAR FRANCK, THE BRIDGE BETWEEN THE HUMAN AND THE DEVAS

1. D'Indy, *César Franck*.

2. Ibid.

3. Ibid.

CHAPTER 21. SCRIABIN, A DEVA-EXPONENT

1. Montagu-Nathan, *Contemporary Russian Composers*, chapter 3.

CHAPTER 23. MOUSSORGSKY AND THE SUBLIMATION OF UGLINESS

1. See Montagu-Nathan, *An Introduction to Russian Music*.

2. Ibid.

CHAPTER 26. THE BEGINNINGS OF MUSIC AND RELIGION

1. See Perry, *The Origin of Magic and Religion*.

CHAPTER 28. THE MUSIC AND CHARACTER OF THE ANCIENT EGYPTIANS

1. See Wilkinson, *The Ancient Egyptians*, chapter V, p. 321.
2. Ibid.

CHAPTER 29. THE GREEKS AND THEIR MUSIC

1. See Dickenson, *The Greek View of Life*.
2. Ibid.
3. Ibid.
4. Ibid.
5. See Naumann, *History of Music*.

CHAPTER 30. THE ROMANS AND THEIR MUSIC

1. Horton, *A History of the Romans*.
2. See Naumann, *History of Music*, chapter XXVI.
3. Ibid.
4. Ibid.

CHAPTER 33. MUSIC AND THE REFORMATION

1. Hawkins, *History of Music*.

CHAPTER 34. THE MUSIC OF THE SEVENTEENTH AND EIGHTEENTH CENTURIES

1. See Naumann, *Music in the History of Civilisation*, chapter XIX.
2. Ibid.

CHAPTER 35. A CURSORY VIEW OF MUSICAL EFFECTS IN ENGLAND FROM THE PRE-ELIZABETHAN DAYS TO THOSE OF HANDEL

1. See Green, *Short History of the English People*.
2. See Davey, *History of English Music*.

CHAPTER 36. THE MUSIC OF THE FUTURE

1. Anrias, *Through the Eyes of the Masters*.
2. Ibid.
3. See Schuré, *The Initiate in the Dark Cycle*, 205, 208.
4. Ibid., chapter X.

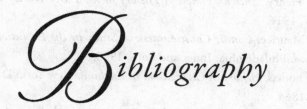

Bibliography

Abell, Arthur. *Talks with Great Composers*. London: Spiritual Press, 1955.

Anrias, David. *Through the Eyes of the Masters: Meditations and Portraits*. London: Routledge & Sons, Ltd., 1932.

Atwood, Mary Anne. *Suggestive Inquiry into the Hermetic Mystery*. Whitefish, Mont.: Kessinger Publishing, 1942.

Bailey, Alice. *Initiation: Human and Solar*. New York: Theosophy Publishing, 1922.

Baraduc, Hippolyte. *Les Vibrations de la Vitalité Humaine: Méthode biométrique que appliquée aux Sensitifs et aux Névrosés*. Paris: Librairie J.–B. Baillière et Fils, 1904.

Baudouin, Charles. *Studies in Psycho-Analysis*. Translated by Eden and Cedar Paul. New York: Dodd, Mead & Co., 1922.

Bedford, Herbert. *Schumann: His Life and Work*. New York: Harpers Brothers, 1925.

Besant, Dr. Annie. *Esoteric Christianity*. Adyar, Madras: Theosophical Publishing, 1914.

———. *Man, and his Bodies*. Krotoma, Calif.: Theosophy Publishing, 1917.

———. *The Ancient Wisdom*. Adyar, Madres: Theosophical Publishing, 1918.

———. *Mahatma Letters to A. P. Sinnett*. Adyar, Madras: Theosophical Publishing, 1923.

Bhagavan Das. *The Science of Peace*. London: The Theosophical Publishing Society, 1948.

————. *The Science* of *the Emotions*. London: The Theosophical Publishing Society, 1900.

Blavatsky, Helena P. *The Secret Doctrine: The Synthesis of Science, Religion, and Philosophy*. London: The Theosophical Publishing Society, 1888.

Bradley, Robert Noël. *Duality: A Study in the Psycho-Analysis of Race*. New York: Moffat, Yard & Co., 1923.

Breasted, James Henry. *Ancient Times: A History of the Early World*. Boston: Ginn & Co., 1916.

Bucke, Richard Maurice. *Cosmic Consciousness: A Study in the Evolution of the Human Mind*. Philadelphia: Innes and Sons, 1905.

Buckle, Henry Thomas. *History* of *Civilization in England*. New York: D. Appleton & Co., 1864.

Challoner, H. K. *Watchers of the Seven Spheres*. London: Routledge, n.d.

Cooper-Oakley, Isabel. *Le Comte de St. Germain*. Milano: G. Sulli, 1912.

Crotch, Dr. William. *Substance of Several Courses of Lectures on Music*. London: Boethius Press, 1831.

Crowest, Frederick James. *Musical Groundwork*. London: F. Warner & Co., 1890.

Davey, Henry. *History of English Music*. London: J. Curwen & Sons, 1895.

Deussen, Paul. *Outline of the Vedanata System*. New York: The Grafton Press, 1906.

D'Indy, Vincent. *César Franck*. London: John Lane, 1909.

Dickenson, Goldsworthy Lowes. *The Greek View of Life*. New York: Doubleday, Page & Co., 1919.

Draper, John William. *History of Conflict between Religion and Science*. London: Henry S. King & Co., 1875.

————. *Intellectual Development of Europe*. New York: Harper and Brothers, 1874.

Eddy, Mary Baker. *Science and Health: With Key to the Scriptures*. Boston: Science Publishing Co., 1875.

Engel, Carl. *Music of the Most Ancient Nations*. London: William Reeves, 1929.

Evans-Wentz, Walter Yeeling. *Fairy Faith in Celtic Countries*. London: H. Frowde, 1911.

Fisher, Dorothy Canfield. *The Montessori Manual for Teachers and Parents*. Cambridge: Robert Bentley, 1913.

Fielding-Hall, Harold. *The Hearts of Men*. London: Hurst & Blackett Ltd., 1901.

————. *The World Soul*. New York: Henry Holt, 1913.

Flagg, William J. *Yoga or Transformation*. New York: J. W. Bouton, 1898.

Fowler, William Warde. *Rome.* New York: Henry Holt & Co., 1912.

Fox Strangways, Arthur Henry. *Music of Hindostan.* Oxford: Clarendon Press, 1914.

Frazer, Sir James George. *The Golden Bough.* New York: Macmillan, 1922.

Goss, Madeline. *Bolero: The Life of Maurice Ravel.* New York: Henry Holt, 1940.

Gosse, A. Bothwell. *Civilization of the Ancient Egyptians.* New York: Frederick A. Stokes Co., 1916.

Green, John Richard. *Short History of the English People.* London: Macmillan & Co., 1880.

Grove, Sir George. *Grove's Dictionary of Music and Musicians.* London: Macmillan, n.d.

Guizot, François. *History of Civilization in Europe.* Translated by William Hazlitt. New York: D. Appleton & Co., 1896.

Hadow, William Henry. *Studies in Modern Music.* London: Seeley & Co., 1893.

Hartmann, Dr. Franz. *Magic, Black and White.* New York: John Y. Lovell Co., 1912.

Hartland, Edwin Sidney. *The Science of Fairy Tales.* London: Walter Scott, 1891.

Haweis, Hugh Reginald. *Music and Morals.* London: Longmans, Green & Co., 1896.

Hawkins, Sir John. *History of Music.* London: Novello, 1789.

Heindel, Max. *The Rosicrucian Cosmo-Conception, or Mystic Christianity.* Oceanside, Calif.: Rosicrucian Fellowship, 1911.

Helmholtz, Hermann von. *Die Lehre von den Tonempfindungen.* Braunschweig: Druck und Verlag Von Friedrich Vieweg und Sohn, 1863.

Hiller, Ferdinand. *Mendelssohn: Letters and Recollections.* London: Macmillan and Co., 1874.

Hinton, Charles Howard. *Scientific Romances.* London: Swan Sonnenschien, Lowrey & Co., 1886.

———. *The Fourth Dimension.* London: G. Allen & Unwin, 1912.

Hodson, Geoffrey. *Fairies at Work and at Play.* London: Theosophical Publishing, 1922.

Horton, Robert Foreman. *A History of the Romans.* London: Rivingtons, 1885.

Hullah, John. *Lectures on Modern Music.* London: Longmans, Green, 1896.

Huneker, James. *Chopin: The Man and His Music.* New York: Scribner, 1900.

Hunt, Holman. *The Pre-Raphaelite Brotherhood.* New York: E. P. Dutton, 1914.

Ingalese, Richard. *History and Power of the Mind.* New York: Occult Book Concern, 1902.

Jinarajadassa, Curuppumullage. *First Principles of Theosophy*. London: Theosophical Publishing House, 1956.

Jung, Carl. *Psychology of the Unconscious.*London: Kegan Paul Trench, 1916.

Keightley, Thomas. *Fairy Mythology: Illustrations of the Romance and Superstitions of Various Countries*. London: W. H. Ainsworth, 1928.

Kilner, Dr. Walter J. *The Human Atmosphere*. London: Kegan Paul Trench, 1920.

Klein Sydney T. *Science and the Infinite: Or Through a Window in a Blank Wall*. London: William Rider & Son, 1917.

Knorr, Iwan. *Peter Iljitsch Tchaikovsky*. Berlin: Harmonie, 1900.

Lawson, John Cuthbert. *Modern Greek Folk-lore and Ancient Greek Religion*. Cambridge: University Press, 1910.

Leadbeater, Mahatma Charles W. *The Hidden Size of Things*. New York: Theosophical Publishing House, 1913.

———. *The Christian Creed*. London: Theosophical Publishing Society, 1904.

———. *The Science of the Sacraments*. Berkeley, University of California, 1922.

———. *The Inner Life: Theosophical Talks at Adyar*. Chicago: The Rajput Press, 1911.

———. *Man Visible and Invisible*. London: Theosophical Publishing Society, 1902.

———. *Invisible Helpers*. London: Theosophical Publishing Society, 1903.

———. *The Other Side of Death*. London: Theosophical Publishing Society, 1903.

Leadbeater, C. W. and Annie Besant. *Man, Whence. How and Whither*. London: Theosophical Publishing Society, 1913.

———. *Occult Chemistry: A Series of Clairvoyant Observations on the Chemical Elements*. Adyar, Madras: Office of the Theosophist, 1908.

———. *Thought-Forms*. Adyar, Madras: Theosophical Publishing House, 1901.

Lecky, William Edward Hartpole. *History of European Morals from Augustus to Charlemagne*. New York: D. Appleton & Co., 1917.

Levi, Elias. *Dogma and Ritual of High Magic*. Translated by Arthur Edward Waite. London: Rider & Co., 1896.

Lidgey, Charles Albert. *Wagner*. London: Dent, 1899.

Liszt, Franz. *Life of Chopin*. Translated by Martha Walker Cook. Boston: Oliver Ditson, 1863.

Marques, Dr. Auguste. *Scientific Corroborations of Theosophy*. London: The Theosophical Publishing Society, 1908.

Mead, George Robert Stow. *The Doctrine of the Subtle Body in Western Tradition*. London: J. M. Watkins, 1919.

Mendelssohn-Barthology, Felix. *Letters from Italy and Switzerland.* Translated by Lady Wallace. Philadelphia: Frederick Lexpoldt, 1863.

Montagu-Nathan, Montagu. *Contemporary Russian Composers.* London: Cecil Palmer and Hayward, 1917.

———. *An Introduction to Russian Music.* London: Cecil Palmer and Hayward, 1916.

Mulford, Prentice. *The Gift of the Spirit.* London: Rider & Co., 1917.

———. *The Gift of Understanding.* London: Philip Welby, 1907.

Müller, F. Max. *Sacred Books of the East.* Oxford: Claredon Press, 1880.

Naumann, Emil. *History of Music.* London: Cassell & Co., 1886.

———. *Music in the History of Civilization.* London: Cassell & Co., 1870.

Newman, Ernest. *Wagner as Man and Artist.* New York: Alfred A. Knopf, 1924.

Newmarch, Rosa. *Life of Tchaikovsky.* London: William Reeves, 1908.

Niecks, Frederick. *The Life of Chopin: Frederic Chopin as a Man and Musician.* London: Novello, Ewert & Co., 1902.

Nohl, Louis. *Life of Beethoven.* Translated by John L. Lalor. Chicago: Jansen, McClurg & Co., 1880.

———. *Beethoven's Letters.* Translated by Lady Wallace. Boston: Oliver Ditson & Co., 1886.

Oxon, M. B. *Cosmic Anatomy Structure Ego.* London: J. M. Watkins, 1921.

Parananda, Sri. *An Eastern Exposition of St. John.* New York: Theosophical Society, 1902.

———. *An Eastern Exposition of St. Matthew.* London: Kegan Paul and William Hutchinson, 1904.

———. *The Writings of Origen.* n.p., n.d.

———. *The Writings of Clement of Alexandria.* n.p., n.d.

Perry, William James. *The Origin of Magic and Religion.* New York: E. P. Dutton & Co., 1923.

Pfister, Dr. Oskar. *Some Applications of Psycho-Analysis.* London: Allen & Unwin, 1923.

Prasad, Rama. *Nature's Finer Forces and the Science of Breath.* London: The Theosophical Publishing Society, 1890.

Prescott, William H. *History of the Reign of Ferdinand and Isabella.* Philadelphia: Lippincott, 1872.

The Puranas.

Ramsay, Dean. *Two Lectures on the Genius of Handel.* London: Blackwood, 1862.

Reissmann, August. *Life and Works of Schumann.* Translated by Abby Langdon Alger. London: G. Bell & Son, 1886.

Rockstro, William Smith. *Mendelssohn.* London: S. Low, Marston, Searle, and Rivington, 1884.

Rolland, Romain. *Handel.* Translated by Dr. Eaglefield Hull. New York: H. Holt & Co., 1916.

Sabatini, Rafael. *Torquemada and the Spanish Inquisition.* London: Stanley Paul & Co., 1913.

Schumann, Robert. *Music and Musicians.* London: William Reeves, 1877.

Schuré, Édouard. *The Great Initiates.* London: Rider & Co., 1920.

Scott, Cyril. *The Initiate.* By His Pupil. London: Routledge and Kegan, 1907.

———. *The Initiate in the New World.* By His Pupil. London: Routledge and Kegan, 1927.

———. *The Initiate in the Dark Cycle.* By His Pupil. London: Routledge & Sons, Ltd., 1932.

———. *The Adept of Galilee.* London: Routledge and Sons, 1920.

Sinnett, Alfred Percy. *The Growth of the Soul: A Sequel to Esoteric Buddhism.* London: London & Benares, 1905.

———. *Super-Physical Science.* Hollywood: Theosophical Publishing House, 1917.

———. *The Occult World: Occultism and Its Adepts.* London: Trübner & Co., 1883.

Steiner, Dr. Rudolf. *Knowledge of the Higher Worlds: And Its Attainment.* Translated by George Metaxa. London: Rudolf Steiner Publishing, 1937.

———. *An Outline of Occult Science: The Way of Initiation.* New York: Anthroposophic Press, 1972.

Strachey, Lytton. *Queen Victoria.* New York: Harcourt, Brace & Co., Inc., 1921.

Svatmarama, Swami. *The Hatha Yoga Pradipika* (fifteenth century).

Tarnowski, Stanislaw. *Chopin: As revealed by Extracts from His Diary.* London: William Reeves, 1907.

Taylor, Henry Osborn. *The Mediaeval Mind: A History of the Development of Thought in the Middle Ages.* New York: Macmillan Co., 1911.

Thiers, Adolphe. *History of the French Revolution.* New York: D. Appleton & Co., 1866.

Thompson, Oscar. *Debussy: Man and Artist.* New York: Dodd, Mead, 1937.

Troward, Thomas. *Edinburgh Lectures on Mental Science.* New York: Dodd, Mead, 1909.

———. *Bible Mystery and Bible Meaning.* New York: R. M. McBride & Co., 1931.

———. *The Law and The Word.* New York: R. M. McBride & Co., 1917.

Underhill, Evelyn. *Mysticism: A Study of the Nature and Development of Man's Consciousness.* London: Methuen, 1911.

The Upanishads.

Valmiki. *The Yoga Vasishta.*

Vivekananda, Swami. *Raja Yoga.* New York: Ramakrishna Vivekananda Center, 1956.

———. *Gnana Yoga.* New York: Ramakrishna Vivekananda Center, 1955.

Von Wasielewski, Joseph Wilheim. *Life of Schumann.* Translated by Abby Langdon Alger. Boston: Oliver Ditson & Co., 1891.

Wagner, Richard "Letter to Röckel," January 25-26, 1854.

———. *My Life.* New York: Dodd, Mead, 1911.

Waite, Arthur Edward. *The Occult Sciences: A Compendium of Transcendental Doctrine and Experiment.* London: Kegan Paul, Trench, Truebner, 1923.

———. *Studies in Mysticism and Certain Aspects of the Secret Tradition.* London: Hodder and Stoughton, 1906.

Walker, Edward Dwight. *Reincarnation: A Study of Forgotten Truth.* London: Ward, Lock & Co., 1888.

Wells, H. G. [Herbert George]. *God the Invisible King.* New York: Macmillan Company, 1917.

Wilkinson, John Gardner. *The Ancient Egyptians.* London: John Murray, 1854.

Woodroffe, Sir John. *The Serpent Power.* Madras: Ganesh and Company, reprint 2003.

———. *Shakti and Shakta.* London: Luzac & Co., 1918.

The Yoga Sutras of Patanjali.

Index

BOOKS OF RELATED INTEREST

Harmonic Experience
Tonal Harmony from Its Natural Origins to Its Modern Expression
by W. A. Mathieu

Harmonies of Heaven and Earth
Mysticism in Music from Antiquity to the Avant-Garde
by Joscelyn Godwin

Harmony of the Spheres
The Pythagorean Tradition in Music
by Joscelyn Godwin

The Soundscape
Our Sonic Environment and the Tuning of the World
by R. Murray Schafer

***The Magic Flute* Unveiled**
Esoteric Symbolism in Mozart's Masonic Opera
by Jacques Chailley

The Power of Sound
How to Be Healthy and Productive Using Music and Sound
by Joshua Leeds

The Secret Power of Music
The Transformation of Self and Society through Musical Energy
by David Tame

Mozart the Freemason
The Masonic Influence on His Musical Genius
by Jacques Henry

INNER TRADITIONS • BEAR & COMPANY
P.O. Box 388
Rochester, VT 05767
1-800-246-8648
www.InnerTraditions.com

Or contact your local bookseller